THE FOCUS OF BELIEF

THE FOCUS OF BELIEF

by

ARNOLD ROBERT WHATELY

M.A. Camb., D.D. Lond.
Rector of Harford, Devon

" *True mystery casts no shadows.*"
HENRY DRUMMOND

CAMBRIDGE
AT THE UNIVERSITY PRESS
1937

CAMBRIDGE UNIVERSITY PRESS
Cambridge, New York, Melbourne, Madrid, Cape Town,
Singapore, São Paulo, Delhi, Mexico City

Cambridge University Press
The Edinburgh Building, Cambridge CB2 8RU, UK

Published in the United States of America by Cambridge University Press, New York

www.cambridge.org
Information on this title: www.cambridge.org/9781107626935

© Cambridge University Press 1937

This publication is in copyright. Subject to statutory exception
and to the provisions of relevant collective licensing agreements,
no reproduction of any part may take place without the written
permission of Cambridge University Press.

First published 1937
First paperback edition 2013

A catalogue record for this publication is available from the British Library

ISBN 978-1-107-62693-5 Paperback

Cambridge University Press has no responsibility for the persistence or
accuracy of URLs for external or third-party internet websites referred to in
this publication, and does not guarantee that any content on such websites is,
or will remain, accurate or appropriate.

CONTENTS

PREFACE

In this all too small compass I have attempted to communicate to others whom it may concern a slight idea of the main results of a long mental process. I have tried to trace the course of several convergent lines of thought that lead, in and for my own mind, to an absolutely focalized view of the Christian creed. My mind has followed spontaneously an ideal of simplicity, unification and concentration, to which not a few others, I suspect, are also groping.

This essay in focalization relates to our understanding of faith no less than of its doctrinal content. If the object of faith should prove to be, in respect of its intellectual commitments, not many things, but one inclusive thing: in other words, if "Redemption" (including all that it directly presupposes) be in itself not a composite but a single idea, then two results should accrue. First, we may expect to find this one dominant idea a master-key for the interpretation of all Christian—and ultimately of all religious—truth. Secondly, faith itself must surely prove far easier to understand and justify than when, however concentrated upon God, it is more or less dissipated among the items of God's Revelation. Its own function being simplified and centralized, its relation to reason and the will assumes a new lucidity.

This is in no sense a short cut to truth. It has taken me decades to find it; and I do not expect it to convey to any other the same satisfaction as to myself. For, since we are different and all fallible, the very quest for a common centre only brings more clearly to light the different mentalities that share it. My own confidence (on the intellectual side) amounts simply to this: that whatever may be wrong in my ideas is, relatively to *my own* perspective, unessential. One cannot impose upon other minds a system of thought that, in one's own mind, shades off into the inarticulate.

And, as before the goal is reached, so afterwards, thought

cannot rest upon its oars. Endless new vistas—therefore new problems—appear, which are hidden till the light is fixed at the centre to which they converge. But, if we have found, each for himself, our own focus in eternity, the old difficulties no longer impinge upon the innermost man. We are anchored where the Inward and the Outward meet, at the *exit in infinitum* of the main currents of thought and life.

But, just because our own personal standpoint cannot be abandoned, there are always limitations to our endeavours to reconstruct for others the general outline of our reflection upon the subject-matter of faith. There may seem to be gaps in my exposition where to me there is continuity. But I think that, where the disposition to sympathetic understanding exists, this will be no case of a chain rendered untrustworthy by weak links. Even in pure philosophy —when it is a matter of vital spiritual interest—surely the thinker works to his Whole from a pre-existing adumbration of it in his own mind. It is the presence of the end at the beginning that is the bond of all that his philosophy contains. And for myself I can truly say that thought is rather a differentiating than a putting together—the taking on of shape, colour, and inter-relation by things seen in a mist. I can only hope that I may prove to have assisted, in some other minds, a parallel process of emergence.

Briefly to allude to my philosophical leanings, I may mention two types of thought—complementary, as I regard them—in each of which my own has recognized a valuable friend. First, the "Phenomenalist" movement, initiated by Edmund Husserl, realistically understood. Secondly, the "regressive" or "serial" mode of thinking, most impressively employed on the Time problem by Mr J. W. Dunne (who sees also its much wider significance) in his book all too modestly entitled *An Experiment with Time*, followed by *The Serial Universe*. May I here venture to allude to an article of my own which appeared in *Mind*, Vol. I, N.S. No. 71, "The Higher Immediacy", wherein is indicated the trend of my

views on the Theory of Knowledge at an earlier stage?
I need hardly say that no writer is to be held committed to
opinions that I, on my side, regard as akin to his.

My own primary interest is in Epistemology rather than
speculation—which is here entirely renounced—and, since
the Theory of Knowledge is part of its own subject-matter,
I can only hope that what I have said about the relation of
reason to faith may be seen exemplified in my own reasoning
throughout.

But, after all, that which gives the focus to a religious
philosophy must itself be outside all philosophy. That is why
it has been almost impossible not to write as on the defensive.
I could hardly expound what Divine Revelation and Redemption mean to myself otherwise than in antithesis to some of
the Liberalism of to-day—or yesterday. My deep sympathy
with the Barthian movement, as with the cognate teaching
of e.g. Karl Heim, has been freely expressed, in spite of
differences. What could be more superficial than to dismiss
it all—or any great religious movement—as a nervous reaction
after the War? The fact is, as it seems to me, that Barth's
teaching reflects a singularly subtle and profound religious
experience, the more notable in that it has elicited the like
in so many minds. It is difficult to criticize him without
spoiling him, and I am under no delusion that I have succeeded
in this myself. But there are certain positions, necessary to
the general context of my thought, which, just because of the
affinity, needed to be set over against his.

The treatise would bear a great deal of expanding, but I
have not risked its fate by this. On the other hand, there is
repetition of the same ideas in different connections, which
needs no apology. Unification of thought requires not only
convergent, but cross, threads; and I hope that some readers
will find more of these than I have displayed.

Lastly, the treatise does not *work up to* the belief in God
or in the Christian Gospel. The whole is posited from the
outset. Some impetus for the quest is presupposed, but no

certainties. But, if the internal unity of Christian doctrine *is* reached, the intellect has won its own vision, and Revelation at the same time its self-evidence. "Dogmas" as such do not come into our theme, only the Gospel of Redemption as the *one* living truth; but dogmas are at least phenomena, and our interpretation of them will radically depend upon our answer to the challenge of that Gospel.

A. R. W.

April 1937

CHAPTER I

INTRODUCTION

It is a significant fact that the theology that stands for the most indivisible and concentrated—indeed the simplest— idea of the Gospel, that of Karl Barth, is among the most revolutionary in method, the most elusive and difficult, the most closely allied, perhaps, to a particular intellectual type. The movement that is charged with disparaging the intellect began in crowded lecture-rooms. But the difficulties are entirely different from those which confront us in the building up of complex systems of thought, and also in our endeavours to rationalize the several "dogmas" of religion, considered as relatively separate problems. This theology works to, not from, simplicity. It is the effort of men, themselves sharing the sophisticated human mind, to re-tread forgotten paths, to turn thought against the pretensions of thought, to place their own thinking under the Cross. The restless dialectic that knows no standing-ground but the perpetual reference to That which transcends its rivals and itself together has its own claim, even as a theology among theologies—a claim based on a truth that applies to thinkers as such no less than to men as such, that "he that exalteth himself shall be abased and he that humbleth himself shall be exalted".

But still the question is not set at rest. Theology remains a body of thought, still incompletely digested and unified in the human mind. If our belief is not to find its own centre of gravity in our own thought, if it is to look ever outward to an objective "Word of God", what shall we say of the interpretation and attestation of this authority? Are we not back in the subjective again? The only answer to this is that the Word of God, under right conditions, must be self-interpreting and self-attesting to our faith. But what is the content of that Word of God that can so elucidate and so verify itself? And, conversely, what precisely is that in us, called faith, to which all the conditions, moral and intellectual, of such a revelation are fulfilled? These two questions are inseparable, and even to propound them is to admit the unique function of faith. The theology that sets itself to find the one key to them does not glorify the intellect—even under the cover of immanental Theism—at the expense of direct belief in an articulate revelation. But it gives it, none the less, its greatest glory, that of surrender—within the total surrender of faith—to its Creator and Archetype.

For, as man is glorified as God's instrument, not as the master and exploiter of His gifts, so human words and concepts are the truest when they serve a revelation that can use them without self-committal to them; when they give the message of a God who speaks in the language of our minds, but who knows no privileged philosophy except that which best clears the way to the Silence where we hear His voice.

But still we must continue to think hard. For even this release of the faith function, on a common basis, is a task that may seem interminable. It may be quite right to look forward to a time when Christians shall really agree upon the essential things and live and work together under the dominance of accepted truth, and when all differences shall have their interplay upon a secondary plane. But the time seems indefinitely remote. We may indeed, as we are advised to do, define our terms; but that method reveals differences beneath our unity, no less than unity beneath our differences. And these differences have roots so deep in the logic and experience that belong to the several types of Christian thought, and to the differing individuals within them, that it is hard to attain to agreement on particular questions without an uneasy sense of superficiality, born of our very success.

The true bond between us, we venture to plead, is to be sought in a more adequate sense of the transcendence of God and of God's truth. For that will mean

(1) an infinite distance, beyond the warring contradictions of our thought,

(2) an infinite penetration, beyond our own ultimate analysis of the terms of our thinking,

(3) an infinite intimacy, that speaks to the heart of the individual beneath the deepest levels of his reasonings with others and with himself,

(4) a future of infinite content, that moves to us rather than we to it—moves to gather us up, ideas and all, on to another plane, and to judge all our thoughts with a refiner's fire.

But here again, when we have grasped all this, the paradox retreats further back. The very conception of God's truth and grace, and of the faith which receives them, which thus humbles the highest achievements of our thought and illumines with hope its darkest perplexities, *is* a conception. It is *our* thought about Him. And, as such, it commits us to much besides. It is itself part of an organic theology. Its connection, in representative writers, with certain views of the various doctrines, with a centrally soteriological interpretation of the Christian religion, with certain conceptions of the Church and of other matters, and with an eschatological orientation, is not fortuitous. If indeed our ideas about Revelation, in itself and in relation to the human mind, govern our interpretation of the content of the message and of the character of the Revealer, we have here again a theology among theologies, a philosophy among philosophies, opinions ranged against opinions. The theology that is to raise us above the conflict seems to take sides within it. For surely the acceptance of the Divine Word as above human ideas does not mean that all are equally true and equally false.

We shall deal with these matters in the succeeding chapters. But meanwhile we submit that such a situation is one that we can accept without any inconsistency. We do not ask for cessation of the interplay, even of the controversy, between the views of different Christians. But, in this very interplay, that line of thought has a peculiar advantage that has the most thorough and satisfying conception of the very meaning of our differences and intellectual perplexities—of the very fact of their presence—in relation to that of Divine truth. That theology is the best that can best explain Theology.

The purpose of intercourse and argument between the types of thought is not directly to reach agreement, but to share what can be shared, to replace division, where possible, by unity, but also confusion by division. That the ultimate meaning of our terms and the perspective of our belief cannot be entirely the same for all, and is often very different, does not discredit this intercourse. It is vital to our fellowship in a common Gospel. This Gospel can have an almost entirely common *language*, if by language we mean words. But human *ideas* also are the language in which God speaks to men, and for no two of us is this language absolutely the same. And we have not yet found an Esperanto.

But meanwhile we press the need and possibility of an *intensive* theology, that in itself is neither empirical nor metaphysical, but penetrates, by spiritual insight under logical control, to the soul and essence of a revealed truth, recognized as such by faith; and thence works outward to interpret in the light of that truth the concentric circles of thought and life. We are one in the Church of Christ, which is the nucleus of a new society with a new social mind; and we need not fear that, in the long run, our honest differences will be barriers. We shall look to the superhuman Truth and the mysterious Purpose, which can be trusted even blindly, because they are hidden behind the revealed glory of the Light of the World.

But, paradoxically, the Theology of Transcendence—the Theology of the Gospel-as-such—tends to be both subtle and also challenging. Subtle because it is an escaping from the mazes—because it accepts the elusiveness of what others treat as ultimate, or at least stable, terms. Challenging because its Gospel is a paradox, not by accident but in essence: because it is compelled to treat much of our accepted thought-construction as in effect impingement and denial; because, more than all theologies, it confesses itself a voice crying in the wilderness "Prepare ye the way of the Lord."

Finally, and above all, there is one thing that is essential if the Divine truth is to make good its claim, and that is *focus*. That found, the many truths are embraced in one Truth. The line of argument before us is inspired by the conviction that, if indeed that Truth can be viewed as an integral and focused whole, we have the key to the understanding, not only of its several elements, but of the meaning, rationality, and grounded assurance of the faith wherein they are apprehended. Then the uniqueness and transcendence of the Revelation, so far from being separative and alien in relation to the general range of thought, only gives a deeper meaning to the union of reason and faith. The old direct one-to-one correspondence between the ideas of religion and those of secular thought becomes a matter of secondary quest. The mutual unity of religious and secular knowledge (not to say of the latter within itself) will now be understood in terms not so much of continuity as of complement: in terms of aspect, sphere, or dimension, according to context. Thus only—not by our system-building—will the universe, one in the mind of the Creator, be apperceived as one by the created mind that has taken definitely the view-point of faith.

To him who has secured this secret a host of difficulties will melt away, like the phantom army that vanished, at the sound of the church bell, from the walls of Prague.

CHAPTER II

FAITH AND THE WILL

Faith in its relation to the will may be regarded in two complementary aspects. To these will be devoted the first two main sections of the chapter.

I

Faith as an *act* of the will. Four points must here be noted.

First, faith is decision; but in what sense? Not in that of the mere "will to believe" of James' famous essay. Here an essential distinction must be borne in mind. On the one hand, regarded from outside itself, it is certainly, as we sometimes put it, a venture:

> Nothing before, nothing behind,
> The steps of faith
> Fall on the seeming void, and find
> The rock beneath.

But, in its internal character, it is not a venture—is not an experiment. It does not, as such and in its own act, take chances. For itself, its object—God self-revealed—is simply *there*, however vaguely apprehended, and however weak and fitful the faith. It appears as a venture when we are thinking *of* faith, not when we are thinking *in* faith. It is not a *venturing*. Its object is not just the theistic hypothesis, but God. That that leads us to the paradox that no one can really understand faith without believing in God we do not for a moment deny. This will appear in other connections later on. Meanwhile we need only affirm that the character of venture, or adventure, which certainly attaches in some sense to faith, is only relative to our reflection upon its place and functions, and does not belong to its inherent spiritual meaning, or to its psychology.

Secondly, as the faith-act is not—essentially and ideally—tentative, so neither is it effort. That belongs to its limitations, not to its strength. Decision of character is attributed to one who always *has* decided, not to one who always *is* deciding. The supreme faith-act, so far as it is truly such, is the abandonment not only of our self-will, but of our self-reliance; and some self-reliance is implied in all effort. Of course, to abandon effort in advance of its supersession by faith is to yield to indifference or despair. But the ideal of volition, even short of religious faith, is to abandon trying in favour of just doing. To will is to act *instead of* not acting, or instead of an alternative act.

(We distinguish the will from the act, however, quite apart from external obstacles to the act, which are here irrelevant: simply because a time-interval may come in between. Will then takes the form of purpose. But this is a secondary, or imperfect form of it; for the interval introduces a situation in which it cannot be pure and direct, and has to be eked out by a self-confidence which human weakness may belie. But more of this later on. Here let it suffice to note that what applies to volition in general certainly applies to the supreme and critical volition of faith.)

Our *third* point has to do with the relation of the will to intellectual sincerity. That the will has an intimate relation to truth is obvious. We may will to face a question with a perfectly open mind, without regard to our own wishes. We may will to admit conviction when we have been trying subconsciously to resist it. But can we really will to believe —which is quite different from testing a hypothesis—before we *see* that the thing is true, and is not the will then superfluous? Can Theology recognize a direct relation of the will to truth, presupposed as such, compatible with intellectual honesty? This brings us to the issue.

Revelation, like everything else that is known or believed, has two sides, content and fact—namely what the alleged object is and the fact that it is; or, as it has been expressed, the *what* and the *that*. Faith is directly concerned with the latter only. It decides the question "Shall I accept this or that?" not "What is it that I am to accept?" The latter is the concern, as we shall see in a later chapter, of intuition. We cannot therefore say that faith rests upon intuition. But intuition—or vision—is both the starting-point of faith and its fruit: before the faith-act, perhaps only an elusive glimpse; after it, a dawn upon the mountain-tops that we stand to watch, growing more and more unto the perfect day. What then does the faith-act do? It *deliberately* focuses that which is glimpsed, listens to that which is at first involuntarily heard. It is not strictly a decision to believe, for belief cannot create itself: it is a decision to look. For, though the vision is a vision of *what* the object is—its content—yet the content itself includes one quality which carries with it the claim to acceptance, namely the offer (if we may so put it) of self-evidence. That faith is also the decision to act upon what is accepted as truth must be affirmed at once. This it is immediately and essentially. And we shall understand this, not by super-adding anything to our idea of faith, but by penetrating more deeply into it. That will be our next point. Meanwhile let us note so far that faith, as a direct inward reaction to a given object, is simply the deliberate adoption of an attitude in which we *see*, really see, for we start from the hypothesis that it is really there.

Faith, then, does not accept an opinion: it accepts a certitude. But this can only mean that the certitude has begun to be such before, or *pari passu* with, the act of faith. This imperfect certitude is not the same thing as opinion. The visible object is there, but shines through a mist. It may begin as a vague feeling, elusive to reflection, of Something confronting us, which reveals itself as we advance towards it. But, however the accepted vision may fail in steadiness or lucidity, all its functions play around a core of absoluteness at the centre, as some of us may even be able to verify introspectively. And it is just this intuitional character of the

Truth that gives occasion to the volition of faith. We cannot will to infer, but we can will to look, and to continue looking.

(But, if the object is given as self-evident, and, if it is, necessarily, an object to faith, and not otherwise effectively known, then the germ at least of the faith that accepts it is also given. The great age-long problem which this creates will be considered before we close this chapter.)

We have been thinking of faith as the definite acceptance of an intimation in some form objectively yet inwardly presented. And this brings us to our fourth point. So far this assertion of the close organic connection between truth and the will—going beyond the recognized commonplaces— may seem paradoxical. But so far truth has been regarded in abstraction from the larger whole to which it belongs. When we understand this, the paradoxes disappear, and, at the same time, we may be in the position to bring some unity into these larger thoughts, in return for the stability and completeness that they will have contributed. The will, as we have so far considered it, has been directed toward God, and yet only in respect of one issue, namely truth. And we have now to ask: "What is the relation of such volitional acceptance to the general range of moral and practical goodness which also is the concern of the Godward will?" In other words, "What is the relation of belief to character?" We can here only give briefly the essential answer, just in order to complete the immediate subject of the chapter. The thread will be taken up in other contexts.

We have first to consider the relation of faith to repentance. Faith, in its concentrated expression, is a Godward volitional act. So is repentance, which is certainly not faith under another name. Thus, if we are to carry through the idea of faith as the supreme Godward activity of the will, we must bring the two as closely together as possible. Now it should not be hard to see that repentance, in its true Christian sense, contains an implication of faith, and that all Christian faith is accompanied by repentance, or at least presupposes it. These two spiritual acts are in fact phases of one act; and repentance, though Godward like the other, is its negative side. Undoubtedly it means, as we are often and rightly reminded, a change of mind and attitude *towards* the good, no less than from the evil. But we have only to remember that the evil from which we turn comprises sloth, indifference, passive selfishness, unresponsiveness towards God, and so forth—that is to say, the evil that is the opposite to positive good—in order to see that the negative definition of repentance (which is really what we mean by the word when we are using and not merely explaining it) includes all that it should include. But the act is a negative act, a rejecting and condemning; and, since the two acts—or phases—are thus different in quality and even relatively separate, it is inevitable that they should be put side by side, as they are in the New Testament. But repentance is not the mere complement of faith, for each is unreal without the other. The full significance of their mutual unity, however, does not appear till our view of the Atonement is determined.

Then (still dwelling on our fourth point) we pass to a second apparently complementary idea, namely self-consecration. This, still more decidedly, is not really complementary; for it is absorbable by that of faith, in a sense in which repentance is not. For the practical and moral conditions of salvation are internal to faith. It is, as Brunner says, a totality-act, and the only one. The most apparently complete self-surrender that is not primarily a faith-act is still only self-diremption. The more closely and severely it descends from the clouds to embrace the concrete temptations and possibilities of actual life, the more it appears as dependent upon a force, a tension, which a given degree of reinforcement of the enemy would break. No critical act—though strangely this is not always admitted—can be predetermined within the nature of him who performs it. Certainly not the faith-act. Its occasion is *crisis*. Here, not before, the soul's life receives its determination. And, just for this reason, it is not an act among acts, but the act behind all acts that are due to the grace of God. This is the *idea* of faith, presenting no adequate phenomena in our temporal lives, yet the key to the innermost interpretation of their victories.

And, if the subjective scope of faith is thus total, so is its objective reference, even when considered simply as the acceptance of truth. We are too apt to disintegrate the meaning of faith, and to forget that, as it is an assent to the proposition that God is: to certain doctrines about God: to the reality of Redemption and grace; so *ipso facto* it accepts a promise of spiritual renewal that is infinitely concrete and personal, relevant to the situation of the moment, and thence moves—inward, outward, and onward—to the motives that govern us and the relations in which we are placed. And it is easy to let these two sides of faith fall apart. For we all know that there may be a merely intellectual belief in Redemption, whereas personal grace must be met by personal faith. But the credential is the same, for, given the personal faith, the two facts are the same. There is no *abstractly* universal salvation.

The Light cannot be without the Life; and, if we know God, we ought to know that we know. And this means knowing ourselves as the recipients of the motives and powers of that Life, albeit only in the germ. And this again means that the surrendered will is itself given to us, even though given in the very faith-act that receives it. For obviously we cannot believe that we have received, or are receiving, the spirit of service and at the same time have no intention to serve. In short, the moral motivation of the will can be defined without residuum, when the context requires it, in terms of acceptance.

We are generally ready to admit that we know by faith what God has done *for* us in the past, what He is doing for us now, what He is offering to us now, what our actual experience now may be *on the condition* of faith. But in each case there is a gap of time, the gap of our uncertain response. The faith that knows God in the very kindling of itself—at this we stumble. But there is no logical break in the Divine action. Its reach must extend in an *unbroken* line from the world to the Ego. It must include—not on a secondary plane—what God *is* doing in us now, and also—and here is the truth in predestination—what God has done for us individually before Time. We shrink from this bold consistency, partly because we fear lest the ethical strenuousness of conscience should suffer. This fear rests upon a narrow conception of the content of faith, both on the Godward and on the manward side.

We may note here a habit of thought that obscures for us the arrest of consistency in our doctrine of faith. We first supplement our idea of grace with that of the necessary human response. *Then* we affirm that this response also is due to grace. Thus grace meets grace from opposite directions. This is relatively true; but, unless it is carefully checked from a more inclusive view-point, it breaks the action of God into two. Whereas it is only the *rejection* by the will that breaks the action of God. We fail to see God's giving *in* our accepting; and so, baulked by this fatal qualification, *sola fides* breaks down.

II

The second main aspect of faith now calls for attention. We have so far regarded faith as an act. But we also recognize other facts—still volitional—about faith; a life of faith, an attitude of faith, the maintenance of faith, and other such concrete realities about it that all, in some way, seem at least to imply continuity. This demands careful understanding by all those who are interested in the Barthian movement, and desire to criticize it without blunting the edge of its primary message. If faith lies only in acts of decision, it would seem to be like the telegraph posts without the wires. For, in the typical Barthian teaching, anything akin to status or possession is rigidly excluded. "To have is to dominate."[1] And this is applied even to the knowledge of God. We know God as the Unknown: or, again, we do not so much know Him as He us. This rejection of what seems to be a necessity of thought is at once too resolute and too paradoxical for facile rejection or revision.

Nevertheless we cannot surrender the continuity of faith, or let it take care of itself. Surely, what we receive from God we *have* when we have received it, or it has not been received: whatever we learn, we know after the learning, or we have not learnt it. And does the idea of having always imply dominance? We "have" many things in the sense of habitually enjoying them, such as fine weather during a holiday. And is not God's possession of us itself—securing our possession in Him of things present and things to come—the greatest thing that we *have*? If joy is permissible in the instant of response to God: if assurance—*God*-given only, as we are earnestly and emphatically told—is really God-*given*, can there be no retention? Or what is the time-limit?

This question of the instantaneousness and continuity of faith brings us close to the problems of Time and Eternity. As this line of thought will appear in other contexts, it may be well to turn our attention to it briefly here.

Where do Time and Eternity touch? Or, in what direction—if any—shall we look for a gap, or gaps, in the *idea* of Time, where it lets in a few rays of light from beyond it? Now continuity and instantaneousness are terms of Time; and, if these are the points of contact, we may the better understand their application to the contact of faith with the Eternal.

Time is succession, but this is not all. Sustaining this conception on either side we find two complementary ideas, each expressed, though always imperfectly, within the tem-

---

[1] "Aber diese Gewissheit ist immer nur punktuell, nur in einem Akte Gottes immer neu anzunehmen, nicht ein haben, dessen man sich freuen kann." A. Keller, *Der Weg der dialectischen Theologie durch die kirchlichen Welt*, p. 22.

poral succession itself. We have already just indicated them, but, in their ideal completeness, we may call them wholeness and punctuality. Each forms a transition-point to the meaning of Eternity.

Wholeness is adumbrated *within* the time-sphere by the "time-span", which has been made much use of in e.g. the philosophy of Royce. The "specious" present, as in music, gathers up a series of sensations into one experience, which transcends their succession, and thus, so far, Time itself. So, on a larger scale, we speak of the present phase of our lives, the present time, and so forth. These time-spans constitute "the present" for us according to the context and purpose of our thoughts. In varying connections, containing and contained periods—the year, the day, or the minute—may be "the present". And all this points to a relatively complete whole—life or history or as the case may be—and ultimately to an absolute whole, as when we say that God sees all time as a whole. But, be it observed, the lesser time-span does not lead our thought directly and without a gap to an *absolute* time-span. The time-span, in proportion as it is realized, suppresses the units that compose it, and has to be dissolved if we wish to grasp them fully: eternity enhances them. (Not to press the point—which would need too long a discussion—that the time-span, unlike eternity, *must* be included in a larger whole.) And yet, as a comprehension of the parts in the unity of the whole, it certainly expresses what Eternity *on one side* means.

To this answers, however imperfectly, the aspect of faith as a *fact about* the believing person, his total attitude. And, since this *is* an aspect of faith as we actually know it, we gain nothing by not including it in our description.

The complementary truth—with its corresponding danger of onesidedness—is that worked out by Karl Heim in his *Evangelische Glaube* and elsewhere, the thought of Eternity as the ideal, indivisible present, glimpsed in the moving present, which, as we think of it, is already past. To this answer the crises of faith, the decisions, surrenders, conversions. In these, likewise, Eternity is glimpsed; but those who would—as it is easy to do—make tabernacles on the Mount of Transfiguration are disillusioned.

Even when we think of these two hints of Eternity together, they do not give us the rounded-off idea that we are prone to seek. But they give polarity to our thinking. They are the posts between which the wire of temporal continuity, disclosed to our reflection, is fixed. Faith touches the super-rational. Reason can point to it: can remove obstacles to our apprehension of it: but cannot walk round it. As faith has no *pure* embodiment in spiritual phenomena, so it has no finished concept in the sphere of thought. But in the spiritual life itself, and to the life in which, though not yet spiritual, the call of faith is sounded, there is no such elusiveness. We do not need to analyse our faith and experience, or faith and feeling, and determine where the one begins and the other ends; for faith ever renews itself, ever draws afresh from the primary Source of life and light. It is not as though we had ever to look *back* and disentangle a lost thread. Faith looks to the self-revealed God, and knows itself only in His light.

This may help us to understand what spiritual experience is and to do justice to its significance, without confusing it with faith. We cannot even speak of (direct) experience of God without bringing to bear our belief in God, for we cannot experience what is not. And we maim the very idea of faith if we do not recognize that it looks to God as not only Giver in the present and in the future, but Giver, in the past, of experiences that have persisted.

For, on the face of it, our experiences do possess continuity, even though they fade, like a tropical sunset, before our eyes. To our reflection they merely present themselves as data for rational inference, but there is more in them than that. They *claim*, at least, to have objective reference in themselves. So, for instance, the "numinous", which Otto has psychologically isolated, and, so far as may be, analysed. If it is not veridical, then it is no neutral subjectivity, but spiritual hallucination—false. And, if it goes, what else does not go with it? Surely the direct value of the more impressive experiences is no measure of the blank created by the discrediting of them.

It is God Himself, assuredly, not any machinery that He has set going, not any after-effect of His action, that is the source of all renewal. But to renew is to make new, not simply to act anew. And there is no real danger of confusing experience with faith if we understand them both rightly. Experience lives in the light: faith penetrates the darkness beyond it. And we walk by faith, not by sight: therefore not by experience, which is dim and distant sight. But we experience the *meaning of the terms* of Revelation. Without this, faith moves in a vacuum.

To sum up this section. Time tends in two directions towards Eternity, intensively and extensively. Or, to put it differently, Eternity partially embodies itself in Time in two separate ways, which are both essentially imperfect, or they would not be two, penetration and inclusion. And faith, correspondingly, has two aspects, both incompletely visible on our temporal plane. On the one hand, it is a matter of crises, decisions, response to flashes of discontinuous revelation. On the other, it discloses itself as a thread of continuity, though, it may be, a sometimes broken thread. Here it adumbrates the spiritual life in its wholeness, as, in the former case, its beginnings, crises, and tangents. So the very proposition "I believe" may be enunciated either as an act of faith or as a communication. In this latter case, it does not mean merely "I am believing at this particular moment", nor yet that I am in the habit of believing as occasion arises, nor yet, of course, that I am consciously performing through life a continuous act of belief. It is an affirmation about myself *simpliciter*. It is the assertion of a condition or quality, not wholly *in* Time, but reflected in the character, stability, and direction of my temporal life. For, within Time, faith is comprehensive as well as punctual, though it is action;

because life itself, centrally controlled, is an act; just as, conversely, all acts, within Time, *take* time.

III

We conclude this chapter with a very important question, that has been the battle-ground of historic controversies, Divine grace and human freedom. We shall see presently how it may be faced from the standpoint of volitional faith. The full meaning and justification of our answer may not appear till consolidated in the general context of our thought, as it develops throughout the book. We approach the question immediately at the crucial point, not where human freedom is dissipated in separate actions, severally regarded, but as exemplified in the summary repentance of an ungodly life as such. For it is just here that human freedom—however displaced by grace in the various movements of an already surrendered will—seems to remain an irreducible factor. If we appeal to an inner sense, we must not wonder that very strong and emphatic answers are given on either side. And it may well seem impossible, except for the most naïve faith, to combine the doctrine of "sovereign grace" with any genuine theory of human freedom.

Apart from religion, philosophers have often stood for a form of individual determinism—self-determinism so-called —that is intended to conserve all the positive meaning of freewill. We entirely reject this opinion, but there is no absolute necessity to devote space here to dealing with it directly. We have here to consider the relation of the human will, not to its antecedent conditions, within or without the individual, but to Divine grace, regarded, by hypothesis, as proceeding from the Creator Himself immediately, and not from these natural conditions.

We may say that human freedom is simply negative in its action—the refusal of grace. But, if the gift of God is re-fusable, there remains, it may be replied, something left out of it which is part of its essence. The choosing of righteousness is part of righteousness; and so, if God gives the offer, must He not, at the last analysis, give the acceptance? Or are we driven back upon an infinite regress? Shall we leave it at that?

We said previously that any view of God's giving in relation to our receiving that virtually regards them as separate facts, while yet allowing that the latter also is due to His grace, virtually disintegrates the Divine act itself. But, supposing we steadily maintain the unity of this act, and regard the refusal of grace as an arrest—or, if not final, a breaking—of the act, then we may well use this regressive mode of thinking. The acceptance of grace is part of the grace—God's will is behind man's. *That* grace itself is still refusable—man's will *confronts* God's. And so *ad infinitum.* This shows at least the co-equal absoluteness both of the Divine gift and of human freedom, even though only by the alternate resurgence of each behind the other. But we can view this relation in a more positive and constructive light.

One of the great ideas that belong to the central meaning of Christianity is that of Creation. We take it exactly as it stands, and recognize no analysis of it except such as exhibits its transcendence of all analysis. Now the essential dilemma of the Christian Will-controversies is not, we believe, diverse from the ancient problem of the One and the Many, which, insoluble in its abstract form, receives from the theistic doctrine of Creation a concrete and dynamic solution. The will is simply the person regarded as willing. A non-volitional person, and so likewise an unfree will, is a self-contradiction. The problem of the Divine will and our wills is the problem —solved, or superseded, for the Creationist—of Being and beings. That is our first step.

But creation is an act; and thus, if we want to use the idea of it for the understanding of a *state* of things—a relation between God and man—we must think of it as an act somehow prolonged, as it were, into this state. In other words, we must think of spiritual advance as creative, and of Redemption—presupposing as it does a breach—as re-creative. Does it not now appear that the doctrine of human freewill—radical and final—is not at all incompatible with that of the Divine sovereignty, in the sense of the unqualified absoluteness of the gift—*as* a gift—of eternal life? If the gift is rejected, its rejection occurs *short of the last stage of creation*, which stage is the perfecting of the new man, re-created in the new Adam. The philosophical irrationalism is absorbed in the irrationalism of thwarted creation, the irrationalism of Sin. Man is created free, but his freedom can only be complete so far as he is created. If the gift is accepted, its acceptance justifies the full joy and assurance of those who see their own accepting included in the accepted gift. For, as the gift guarantees the Giver (for it is Himself), so also it sets its seal to the real being and creaturehood of the recipient, as a unit—will and all—of Reality. Creation is revealed to him as containing the promise, not conditional but absolute, of the consummation of God's promise for him. Absolute, not because it is not in itself resistible, but because the spiritual apprehension of it means *ipso facto* that it is accepted. Thus, in contrast to older views, prevenient grace is not so much a ground of assurance as an element in it.

And now it should be clear that this view of grace and freedom only holds good if we regard the supreme act of freedom as a totality-act of faith. This alone takes us to the basis of creaturehood. To understand freedom in the light of creation is to understand it in terms of the individual as such and as a whole, as the surrenderer and as the surrendered. We have tried to show that it is only in and through faith that this freedom finds expression. And it is in the new vision attained by this *volte face* that all things—and all concepts—become new. The new creation and the old are fused—fused without confusion, because the meaning of the fusion itself is known to us only in the victorious restoration of the old by the new. It is only in the regeneration of thought that the regeneration of man, who is the owner of the thought, can be understood.

2-2

It may help us if we regard this mode of arriving at our conclusion over against the old extreme doctrine of Election, which seems to agree with it on the Divine side of the antithesis. Election, in the sense of limited predestination, is a wedge thrust in between the old and the new creation, a *tertium quid* that does not link but divides them. Redemption fulfils the meaning of creation, and there could be no half-creations, to be left unfinished. And so—approaching from the other end—it is precisely because the mind, in the light of the new creation, harks back *directly* to the old, that it realizes that unity in difference of finite and infinite Being, *and so of the finite and infinite will,* that is of the essence of creation, and is coherent only as so understood. And it is realized dynamically in the Divine Act of Redemption, in which the Divine creative act is restored.

The appropriation of the will by the Creator is *ipso facto* its emancipation; and that relatively, in the end, even to the Creator Himself; because the goal of its freedom is the perfect spontaneity that transcends mere submission, even to the Highest. The gift of the new life, regarded in the light of its ideal, throws into vivid relief the entity of the recipient, whom God, in creation, has differentiated from Himself.

The old Platonic and pre-Platonic problem of the One and the Many could have no final solution, because it was static and abstract, held apart from the actual world of concrete experience. The truth of the New Creation claims to be a truth of experience and fact.

CHAPTER III

FAITH AND REASON

We have now to deal with the relation of faith to two other elements of our mentality, first reason, then intuition. By thus holding them apart at the outset we shall be the better able to understand their relation to each other and to religious faith. We treat of intuition in the next chapter.

If we begin with the question "What is reason?" it must not be thought that we are setting, off-hand, a huge problem that would require a treatise to itself. We shall attempt only such an answer as will be relevant to the general subject before us, and help us to understand the relation of reason to faith. Two main thoughts meet us at the threshold.

I

First, the key to the meaning of reason—that is, to the door that confronts us at our present angle of approach to it—is *self-consciousness*. A self-conscious being is a rational being. Not, of course, that everyone is always explicitly self-conscious when he reasons. But he *is* conscious, implicitly at least, of his own mind as over against the object-world, even over against itself as included in that world. And this consciousness must tend to become explicit as reason moves forward. Reason, whatever else it is, must be regarded as the taking into account of the personal equation. For it refuses to accept first impressions, or assumptions, including negative assumptions, at their face-value. It says of all ideas "This is an idea, therefore not necessarily the reality itself": nay more, "This is *my* idea, and therefore to be checked from a view-point as impersonal as I am able to attain. I am but one among others." This very discounting of self is a supreme achievement of self-consciousness.

The implication of self-consciousness becomes more and more evident as thought penetrates to its deepest intellectual basis, that is, in philosophy. That even so it is not always applied by the thinker to his own thought: that he does not always ask: "What is the significance for my philosophy that it is just *my* philosophy?" this only means that the last step back in reflective detachment is not always taken.

This may seem to ignore the positive and constructive side of reason, and to treat it as merely critical. But the apparently negative function is at the root of all work of discovery and construction. For the direct mental grasp of what is new is not the task of reason, but of intuition, with which we shall deal later. A new idea, or piece of knowledge, however rigidly deduced from what is already in the mind, enters as such from without. Reason works for new intuitive experience, and its tasks are set by experience. In itself it is simply our reaction to, and quest of, experience, with at least an implicit consciousness of what we are doing.[1]

Reason, then, rests upon self-consciousness, upon the mind's understanding of its own thoughts, as over against the data that are given it to think about. And this amounts, as it develops, to clear introspection; finally to the knowledge, not only of our mental processes, but of *ourselves*. Now Christianity has its own goal of self-consciousness, more fundamental than any other, if not so self-exalting. It is expressed in the "I, yet not I" of St Paul. It likewise claims to *give*—what reason can never find—the view-point from which the true meaning and position of the "self" of each one of us may be seen by himself. If this claim is made good, it holds the key to ultimate rationality in its hands. If so, faith is at once super-rational and rational.

Reason in itself is discontinuous. When the mind accepts spontaneously a statement heard or read, the character of belief at the moment is definite and unique. But, as a state or attitude of the mind afterwards, belief presents a further

[1] See *An Idealist View of Life*, by S. Radhakrishnan, ch. IV.

problem. We do not, and cannot, renew each time the arguments and intuitions to which it owed its existence at the first. How then does belief sustain itself?

The actual working answer to this is that it turns in upon itself and rests upon itself. We believe that we believe, and so *ad infinitum*. We remember the fact of our forming the judgement, and we see no reason to think that, in the same mental situation, the judgement would not be the same. And besides, we retain some sense or experience of belief, bound up with a certain ready-to-hand, if imperfect, reminiscence of the factors that produced it. Again, we act upon our beliefs, more or less, and this tends to fix them. But, granted all this, the retention of our beliefs is a problem in the abstract, and, for the critical philosophy of religion, a very concrete problem. It means that, unless the original judgement is actually renewed in full vigour (and that cannot be done all the time), the new question of the *fact* of our belief itself is liable to arise—a question that could never arise in the act of forming it—and, once the spectre is raised, we shall not easily lay it again. The self-consciousness of reason has advanced a further stage.

And thus a second question has arisen. The first was "Is it true?" The second is "Do I believe it?" And this, though the answer converges with the answer to the other, looks in quite a different direction. We may ignore the challenge, or we may renew the belief on the old grounds, or we may accept the challenge, or at least be troubled with it. Certainly it seems to press with disturbing insistency upon the modern mind. That my beliefs are just *my* beliefs is, as we have seen, the very *raison d'être* of reason. But it is no less its embarrassment. The modern mind doubts not only about what it ought to believe, but about what it does. The question to-day has diffused a mental vapour which obscures the answer to the primary question. The peculiar type of self-consciousness quickened by Psycho-analysis can never be stifled by doubts and criticisms respecting Psycho-analysis itself, and we can only be secured against its depressing and obscuring effects by working through to the other side. For, after all, it is necessary that the human mind should pass through this stage.

This indirect, or reflective belief—belief in our belief—is quite justified, and quite necessary, in its own place. But it throws us back upon an infinite regress. For the conclusion that we reach as to what our beliefs are is itself a new belief, that may call for a like revision. This sets us upon the quest of a deeper basis, a form of belief that is direct, and yet does not vanish as such when the first flash of mental assent is over.

Such belief is faith, and finds its true form when its object is God. It is essentially direct, and quite different from the formation of an opinion. At the same time, it *includes* reason. For, by the very meaning of its Object, it readjusts our relation to the world in which we live, external and mental alike, and rationalizes the very centre of the mind and life that are pivoted upon it. It is the knowledge of God as related to self, therefore the ideal of self-knowledge. The personal equation, therefore, does not throw doubt upon the central faith, or upon the contiguous truths that owe their stability to it; for the *person himself* is drawn into focus. He knows that he knows, for he knows where he stands in the universe.

II

We have dealt with the relation of reason to belief on the side of the believing subject. We have now to consider it on the object-side. All belief, and therefore disbelief, of any kind, has as its background what we may call cosmic faith, the tacit acceptance of an all-embracing Reality, the universe without us and within, as understood and assumed by the given individual. Even this he *may* doubt, if he is a philosophical or pathological sceptic; and his doubts are real when and in so far as his mind is occupied with them, but only so. All denials or doubts that are not mere feelings presuppose belief in this universe-as-it-is-for-me. Here we have a belief that is at once implicit, operative, and continuous, and yet does not need to be justified, for it is the guarantee and criterion of everything else.

How imperfect the recognition of this plain truth is may be illustrated by the very existence of such a problem as the following: "Why do we expect the sun to rise to-morrow morning?" That is, why do we expect the continuance of events that happen in regular sequence? Hume says that we have no true reason, only habit. But this calls for a preliminary question that takes us deeper. On which side does the burden of proof lie? The rising of the sun may be regarded either as a *breach* of the continuity of experience (this is what the form of the problem itself implies) or as the persistence of it. The night goes on till the prolonged experience of its darkness is broken by the first appearance of light. This being a breach, why, we are asked, do we expect it? And it is rightly pointed out that to justify our trust in the continuity of experience by an appeal to that continuity is a *petitio principii*. But, from the other point of view—that of common sense—its failure to rise would be the breach. For this would snap the continuity of that experience of alternating day and night which, even apart from science, is still in possession. We believe that it will rise because we know no reason for its not rising. To which side does the *prima facies* belong? Which is the fundamental continuity? Is life, even at the starting-point of Philosophy —even with the highest hopes of soaring above this level— primarily a series of sensations? Are not life and the universe —however incoherent to us till our thoughts have brought some order into them, however uncertain till we have settled our account with Scepticism—the real starting-point for Philosophy? Philosophy is part of life, and ought it not to look, from the outset, to the rock from which it was hewn?

This cosmic faith, as we have called it, is not itself religious faith, but points towards it and is taken up into it. Just because faith in God finds in Him the lordship of life, self, and the world, it has preoccupied the very sphere from which doubt arises. For in saying that we reject or doubt an idea because of our cosmic faith, that is, because it does not seem to fit into our universe, it is not meant that we *argue from* this incompatibility. There is no inference. This sense of incompatibility is just what doubt and disbelief *are*. And so, when we say that a certain view of the universe is involved in the faith-view of God, we are not referring to any conscious theory, but to an *implication* of theistic faith. Cosmic faith is the ground and sanction of all reasoning, its inarticulate *a priori*, till God unconsciously assumed becomes God revealed. That which was ever behind, beneath, and above thought and life is at last face to face: the Godward life of worship and service can begin.

And then it is that a new element comes into faith, namely trust. Faith consists of these two elements, belief and trust. Certainly they are fundamentally one: but we cannot appreciate the significance of this oneness unless we are quite clear as to the contribution of each term. We *believe* in God's existence and in certain qualities as His. Trust, on the other hand, is a Godward attitude that *presupposes* His existence and qualities. The illuminating paradox of the fusion appears in that the logical priority of the one to the other is lost in the synthesis of faith—that each completes its own essential meaning by union with the other.

All belief, as we have seen, has as its background an assumption of a rational cosmos, and it is this assumption that is transmuted by Revelation into faith in God. But the cosmos is impersonal, and God is personal. Reality, simply as such, calls for no personal relation, nor does such belief in God as merely *rests upon* cosmic faith instead of appropriating and transforming it. But belief becomes radically different—different in its characteristic momentum—when it is confronted by the personal Object. It is Godward: it has become trust.

Trust equally passes into belief. No longer does it receive the second-hand material of opinion, but goes down into the depths of the Divine Revelation, and so accepts on their deepest ontological ground the fidelity of His love and the immutability of His promises.

III

A few words are necessary on the subject of doubt. These will follow easily from what has been said already. If the new divine experience is really focused at the centre of life, and therefore, for the thinker, at the centre of thought, it is clear that doubt, even in respect of things that are not at the absolute centre, is in a far weaker and less dangerous position. We have now a criterion by which we can separate the essential from the unessential and rescue the substance from the form. Reason, once confronted by direct central faith, is in a new situation. Its whole field, itself included, is now dominated by an experience of Reality that was previously latent within it. A datum has come to it which is too integral to be taken to pieces, and too comprehensive to be starved by isolation.

We are accustomed to speak of the surrender of the outworks of our creed, while the citadel remains impregnable. This familiar metaphor gains force when we think of the citadel, not simply as some privileged doctrine or doctrines, but as the Absolute of all doctrines, which receives into safety all our real values, and to which the advance of the surrounding enemy only drives us inward. Religious doctrine is the shock-absorber between reason and faith.

The naïvely religious attitude towards doubt is to treat it as alien yet subjective; outside us as an invader to be overcome, inside us in contrast to the solid reality that is not affected by our misgivings. And yet, on the other hand, true religion bids us to be intellectually honest, and at all costs loyal to truth. This dilemma, where we now stand, is transcended. Belief and open-mindedness certainly pull in opposite directions, but in such a manner as two persons might pull two entangled boughs of trees, to wrench them apart. The eternal element and the discarded elements separate through this very stress, deadly though it may seem.

That is not to say that *this* proposition may be assigned to the one and *that* proposition to the other. It may even be that the same proposition is an eternal truth in the context of my own thought which is untrue as an opinion claiming validity in the general context of the mental world around me. The trueness of propositions—though not Truth in itself—is relative to purpose. This statement may be illustrated from ordinary intercourse. The proposition "There's a star", when it is really a planet, is mainly untrue if we are talking astronomy, mainly true if we are looking for a break in the clouds on a rainy night. And that this is not merely a matter of terminology may be seen by supposing that the speaker would have said "planet" if he had known it to be a planet.

Truth, in this sense of trueness, moves in an ellipse rather than in a circle. This is in substance Otto's doctrine of "ideograms". The two foci are what he calls "conceptual" truth—which is social, arguable, capable of credal formulation—and private truth, which is true because it best expresses God to the given individual mind. Conceptually, the same proposition may be on the whole (though not wholly) untrue, because it conveys to the general mind more serious error than valuable truth, and yet be true as an "ideogram", that is, true to myself, because, *for me*, the balance is on the right side. In the one case the error is vital, the truth incidental: in the other, *vice versâ*. Or—if we may put the antithesis bluntly without being misunderstood—I may think the proposition, but not say it. But all the while the truth-standard outside us and the truth-standard within us are in interaction, and contribute to the genesis and vitality of one another. Truth—in this sense—is for each of us an ellipse, not a plurality of circles, any more than one only.

For, of course, all the time, I am a social being. Only as

such, surely, could I think at all. And it would not be well to cling unnecessarily to formulas that would fall to pieces in the social intercourse of different minds. We must think, so far as we can, in the language of the community. But it is a great gain if we can, theoretically, distinguish between these two motives for rejection or acceptance of doctrinal statements, the personal and the social. We shall not then allow our deeper spiritual experiences either to starve and wilt or to grow rank and wild for lack of intellectual enrichment or of intellectual discipline. We shall be able to use explanatory formulas without becoming their slaves. We shall respect the convictions of our neighbour, even in controversy, because perhaps no correction of them that *we* could ever offer would leave intact things known in his heart and not in ours. We shall shun superficial proselytism. And, at the same time, we shall be guarded against equally superficial eclecticism, because we shall understand better the unformulated truth that is shielded by negative formulas.

Above all, we shall have overcome the dire dilemma: rational intelligibility or spiritual certitude? For we shall know now that God's Revelation needs not to be inarticulate, even when most inward and personal, and that Truth itself lives by the interaction of believing minds. Not in this life will the two foci of the ellipse coincide in the perfect circle, and Truth come to its own in the unity of all in God.

CHAPTER IV

FAITH AND INTUITION

I

The general relation of intuition to reason has been briefly noticed in the previous chapter. It is not a special faculty of knowing. It is all knowing, considered apart from the mental processes by which knowledge is sought, sifted, communicated and guarded from error.

Intuition has long been unpopular with philosophers. It has seemed to carry—as it often does carry in popular speech—a claim to direct and infallible authority, to which other people are expected to defer. Or, at least, it is an organ for the discovery or test of truth which offers some measure of exemption from rational questionings. As such, its pretensions are distrusted as individual and subjective. To appeal to intuition seems to be either presumption or a counsel of despair.

Now, in the first place, the "appeal to intuition" covers an ambiguity. No record of its successes, however impressive and recent, can be more than the ground of an argument. We may say "I am seldom or never wrong in my intuitions, and therefore I feel sure that I am right in this particular instance." But this is only inference: we are using the *fact* of our intuitions as evidence for the confirmation of our own mind, much as we might use it for the confirmation of other minds. The real authority of intuition lies in the intuiting itself. And its use when we are trying to convince another person is to get him to *see* the thing as we see it.

This is a distinction very important to bear in mind. But still the awkward claim to infallibility is not entirely set at rest. For apparent intuitions often prove wrong; and, if we say that they are only intuitions if veridical, how shall we distinguish the true from the counterfeit until after the event? For intuition is more than mere feeling. It has the nature of insight, and ought not to require credentials.

But, after all, it may be said, insight is not generally considered to carry with it infallibility, and yet its value is recognized. Taking intuition in this way, there would be nothing infallible about it, and yet we could value it, as indeed we often do, as an effective, but not unerring, faculty. Sight itself is no more than that.

But then, on the other hand, sight is not in itself liable to error. It sees what it sees absolutely, even in hallucination. Sometimes it is said that such an object is simply "in" the mind. We do not think that this explains anything, but, at any rate, if we *are* driven to say that the phenomenon before the mind is yet only in it, we are trying somehow to find it a home: we are telling where it "is". Now the same must apply, *mutatis mutandis*, to intuition; and surely it concerns us first to enquire what it is that it thus directly grasps, before we ask what its relation is to faith.

The modern "Phenomenalist" movement, initiated by Edmund Husserl, is devoted to a searching examination of this intuitional side of knowledge. It develops the indubitable truth that the inward meaning or essence (*Wesen*) of every conceivable object presented to the mind—including its own contents—is met by a direct act of mental penetration, or, as it is called, "intention", which answers the question "What is it?"[1] In other words, we do not arrive at our knowledge simply by subsuming sense phenomena under classes and universals: every object of thought, psychic or material, is itself and as such a phenomenon—but note, a phenomenon in a fuller and deeper sense than as we ordinarily use the term—a direct object not only of sight, or intro-

[1] "Phänomenologische Darlegungen sind niemals Definitionen, sondern Darstellungen des in Erfahrung gebrachten, des in einer irgendwie gearteten Anschauung zugänglich gemachten Phänomens." A. Metzger, *Der Gegenstand der Erkenntnis*, p. 8.

spection, or memory, as the case may be, but of insight. The mind reaches the interpretation of the meaning of the phenomenon by penetrating to its seat within the phenomenon itself. It is as when we say, in reply to an explanation, "I see". The application of this as a conscious scientific method in various directions has had notable results. And surely the demand it makes discredits our mutual misunderstandings and our superficial concordats. How has the lack of *Wesenseinsicht* both embittered and enfeebled controversy !

Now this insight can only become valid for others so far as we can get them to share it. But we have also seen that there remains a certain difficulty in regarding it as authoritative, when its authority is, as it were, shut up within itself. And here we come to the point. The Phenomenological method definitely and deliberately suspends the whole question of the truth and reality of the objects it handles. It is concerned as such entirely with *what* the phenomenon is, not with the truth of what it conveys. These two questions are, in the long run, inseparable. This inseparability is, in fact, at the root of our conception of religious truth and knowledge. But it is best to suspend the question of truth pending a deeper understanding of the meaning of that which claims it.

There are many ideas—even controverted ideas—that we need only to understand in order to believe. And to a religion that claims absoluteness this in a special manner applies—if the religion is true. Those who believe it can claim that its essence, if adequately exhibited, discloses its own self-evidence. The essence of the Truth is the essence of all truth: there is no abstract truth-standard outside it. We are thus brought round to the conclusions of the preceding chapter. But we may here further note how, if reason simply leads us from insight to insight—that is, works *from*, *towards*, and *for* our direct apprehension—a link has been supplied to us which should make it easier to understand the relation of Revelation to reason. For reason depends at every point upon that which is revealed—or "given"—to it, and the insight—or intuition—that accepts it. In ordinary matters, we think only of reason on the one hand, and the "given" on the other. But if, abandoning the Kantian standpoint, we boldly affirm that reason itself requires a rational subject-matter, *given* to it, then we are readier to understand how an articulate revelation—that is, neither mere feeling nor mere ideas evolved from the human mind—can *go to meet* the mind of man and illuminate it, collectively and individually, with its own light.

The English word "meaning" should help us with this thought. It is a term of consciousness and purpose, not that of the apprehending mind, but that of the mind to which the apprehended idea is referable. We apply it indeed to impersonal objects: we speak, for instance, of the meaning of a situation. Indeed we may ask whether there is not here an intimation of a Mind behind all objects. But, since our aim is not directly apologetic, let it suffice to say that the most significant use of the word—that in which the "meaning of meaning" is explicit—is made when we refer to the meaning that another mind endeavours to convey to us. Here reason outside us makes its claim upon the reason within us.

And the relation likewise of Revelation to faith considered as will may be resumed in this new context. The truth-claim that ideas hold within them is sometimes such as to carry our minds by storm. It might seem that Divine Truth ought above all other so to vindicate itself. But no. Its call is to the innermost central man, which cannot be merely passive, and is not evoked by an overwhelming force. The response may indeed take the form of an immediate and glad surrender, but its essence is crisis and decision, whether our imperfect experience and reflection disclose this essence or not. The Gospel is the supremely Rational, but reason in the deepest things is not, and cannot be, coercive. The "given" Truth —which is the voice of the Giver—calls for an explicit and volitional assent, the assent of the "that" to the "what", which proceeds from the integral man—rational and all else that he is. The call to belief and the call to service are not two things but one thing. And here it is that the significance of Intuitionalism comes in. Just precisely because faith is so definitely volitional, and likewise so central and inclusive, it cannot merely clinch our own opinions, however lofty and spiritual, or merely decide to carry them out in practice. Opinion is secondary, abstract, tentative, specialized. Faith can only accept the self-presented. *What* that is we see, or intuit. *That* It is we believe. And although what It is includes its *necessary* place in relation to our own minds —and so its truth—yet this truth is only implicit in the vision, and can only become explicit by an explicit act of faith.

II

We shall now seek to vindicate the religious significance of intuition, so understood, first as against rationalistic theory, and then against a one-sided anti-rationalism.

It is urged against the Barthians that, when they set Revelation against rational construction, they are shackled by the Neo-Kantian limitations of their philosophy. Reason, it is said, does not indeed construct truth, but none the less, it discovers it, and, in this capacity, why should it be set in antithesis to Revelation, which can use it as a God-given instrument? It might be pointed out that constructive function is often attributed—and in a relative sense correctly —to reason, and that they are right in warning us against surrounding this process with a divine halo. But let us give the objector the advantage of the more effective counter-claim. Let it be granted that reason does *find* truths, and truths bearing on religion. Where then does God come into the process? At two points. He is present "immanently" in the human mind, and He is present as the object of the quest and the discovery. There is relative truth in this. But in neither case, nor in both together, do we reach the idea of revelation. In the one God is the lantern, in the other He is the "find". He is not self-revealed. We *find* Him, however Divine our equipment for the search. Two impersonal aspects of God are brought together, and they are not made personal by combination. What reason finds for us, reason gives to us; and the supreme Word that God has spoken to us by His Son—if indeed He has spoken it—gives itself: it is articulate as it comes from His mouth. It addresses itself, not to inference, but to attention and to faith. Reason may remove barriers, as may also circumstances or the imagination. It may admit the light into its own darkness, the key into its own lock: but it is not the voice of God. Revelation is rational *ex post facto*: it comes as a Gospel.

We cannot agree with those who class Phenomenology with other merely human theories, that stand in contrast to the Word of God as such. Without this *insight into essence* which it expounds, we fail to complete our understanding of faith and reason over against one another. Without the common field, both would perish *in vacuo*. For, with all the limitations and distortions of the human mind, God speaks *to* it, and, if it cannot construct, and cannot find, His final truth, it can *hear* it. Faith cannot make its decision without knowing what it decides upon. There is no clash. The correlate of faith is truth: the correlate of intuition is meaning. True, we apprehend meaning by the Spirit of God; yet the subjective event is the same. God does not reveal the Gospel to a stone or a dog. Intuition is not a means whereby we know the Revelation: it is our knowing of *what* the Revelation is. And the Holy Spirit does not know *instead of* us.

Intuition is the antipodes of explaining away. Its quest is for the meaning and essence of what is there—where it is given, as it is given. It points to the self-revealing object, and, when we have looked, it says "Look closer". It cannot, any more than can our discursive reason, find God. But it is the ear that hears Him, the eye that sees what He shows. We speak of "given" facts, of data, and so forth: they are just there, and we find them. But God is not merely given: He is self-given.

Reason, unless it is definitely prepared to face the challenge

3-2

of real revelation—that is, the communication of a new
object—unique, individual, unpredictable—must always tend
to explain by explaining away. It can never rise above its
source. It is never entitled to deduce, even from the most
exalted discoveries, "This must be God's voice", for a voice
is not deduced, but heard.

But we have also to deal with intuition in reference to an
anti-rationalistic position. We refer to the agnostic strain
apparent in typical Barthian assertions. God is "known as
the Unknown", or only "indirectly", that is, through the
Cross and the Word. That God is, nevertheless, God: that
His Name is not an empty symbol like x, could, of course,
never be denied. It is not just the subject of an impersonal
verb; as if we could say "It redeems", just as we say "It
rains". But, if so, why be so anxious to substitute God's
knowledge of us for our knowledge of Him? This truth is
infinitely significant on its own plane, but it does not touch
the necessary correlation between God's communication
and the mind that receives it.

As to "direct" or "indirect" knowledge, there is a question
we may ask both of the Barthians and of the Rationalists.
How, in spite of current language, is knowledge, as distinguished from the way in which it is obtained, and apart
from all its inadequacies and working approximations, ever
anything but *pro tanto* a direct relation? We do not forget
the distinction between "acquaintance" and "knowledge
about". But, if our relation to God is personal, as is rightly
insisted, then it is certainly acquaintance. The mystery of
personality is that it is *too* intimately known to be defined
or described.

Mysticism, so far as it is the projection of the "God
within"—the cult of the God within *as such*—is rightly
rejected. And this no doubt may take many subtle forms,
against which we cannot too carefully guard ourselves. But
the eye of the sane mystic, whatever his defects, is mainly
directed to the Transcendent, and his temper is self-negating.

And this must not be regarded as all a cover for self-reliance and subjectivism. No doubt we may be deluded into treating our very self-negation as an asset; but, even so, something of its genuine quality may remain; and, as such, it should be respected, whatever baser elements may be mingled with it. The charge of "Pietism" has been made against the Barthians, as hugging their own particular form of faith, and treating other believers as if in darkness. Even this unjust complaint would lose whatever colour of truth it has if their doctrine of faith were applied more generally—or known to be so applied—in sympathetic analysis of existing forms of faith, and not too exclusively associated with challenge and sharp antithesis.

III

And now, having arrived at this stage, we may conclude the chapter by reviewing compactly our attempt to do justice alike to faith and to reason. Intuition is the inseparable complement of each, and so the bond between them. (We have used also, almost as synonyms, the words "experience" and "insight", determined by shades of emphasis, receptivity in the one case, function in the other.) Faith in its imperfect form—the belief in an intuited cosmos or Whole—is the ground and presupposition of all reasoning. This belief tends, as the human mind advances, to grow uneasy about itself, and to satisfy its unrest with foundations that are only relatively stable, if at all. At the level of faith, especially in its full Christian sense, belief no longer rests upon a foundation that is only a reduplication of itself, but feels the solid ground beneath its feet; for its universe of thought and experience—the source no less of doubt and disillusionment than of knowledge and opinion—is gathered up with it on the new foundation.

This gives us the key to the problem how to reconcile reason and faith. What here concerns us is the actual reasoning process of finite man, not the abstract ideal Reason that comes into court with all the prestige of its *ex hypothesi* infallibility. Faith is human faith, and it needs only to adjust its claims with *human* reason. Now it is a simple matter of fact that human reason and the message addressed to faith—however we may interpret that message—do often clash, even where reason has high ideals and is guided by much true insight. But the obstacles it raises belong to the general complex of obstacles, individual and social, that deflect the soul to rejection, error, and obscuration. The Gospel meets this total movement of the human mind, intellectual and non-intellectual, *vertically* (as the Barthians say). It descends with a new call to face a new situation. In this call reason itself is included. But reason cannot submit to mere authority —the judge of which must be itself—but to a new fact, a new vision, a new task. This control from without is, of course, a general law. But here the call is to the free surrender of reason *as a whole*, and therefore also of the larger personal whole to which it belongs—surrender to the creative and Archetypal Reality which holds the key to the meaning of its life. Its new start is but one side of the personal regeneration in which "all things are become new".

Reason has now to undo some of its own work. We have now to accept the relativity and transitory worth of its accommodations to the secular thought of the hour: boldly to meet the old thought and the new alike with paradox, the paradox of a new Fact, that calls our judgement itself into judgement.

There is no disparagement of the true claims of reason in all this. Reason in its abstract infallibility is not suspended for a moment by this call of Revelation, only human reasoning, and that only to be taken up again, under new conditions certainly, but at the point at which it left off. And it does not matter that this vertical impact of Revelation is only partially expressed in the psychological and biographical phenomena: conversions, crises, sacramental acts, new experiences. We are dealing with those *essential* meanings and relations of ultimate ideas that, on the level of temporal experience, are only glimpsed.

This is a form of the *Credo ut intelligam* doctrine of faith. Faith is non-rational in this sense only: that it is an act *sui generis*, and that reason is related to it as one side of that totality of our nature which is the subject-matter of the Redemptive Word and Work to which faith commits us. In the individual person, if he is not strictly a philosopher, or does not realize adequately the implications of philosophy, rational process may seem very little altered. But, when we are considering, as we are here, the relation of faith to human reason at large, it is imperative to take into account this lack of focus, of clue, of compass, which can only be discovered and admitted when it has been made good. It is remarkable how little thinking, even serious and solid, looks for its own *ultimate* standard and justification.

Credo ut intelligam. And yet we often need to say "Intellige ut credas". For, as a simple matter of fact, reason helps to make faith possible. This dependence is, of course, relative to our human point of view. Yet we cannot leave it out of account. But reason only clears the way because it has blocked the way. We know that faith does not always come to us like a bolt from the blue: that obstacles, not only intellectual, are too strong for its initial impact, which yet prevails if they are removed.

If we, then, take these two concepts, reason and faith, in their ultimate and absolute distinctness, we note that reason has a double relation to faith: it precedes it and follows it. That it precedes faith, in the above sense, is indubitable: for we know that ideas and arguments do sometimes facilitate the entrance of faith. And it also follows, in that faith claims its service, and progressively extends its dominion over it, as over the whole man. But the question how far, in any given case, it is the precursor of faith militant, and how far the servant of faith triumphant, is otiose. The distinction is wanted for the analysis of the idea, but not for the sorting of the facts.

The final ground for the understanding of faith is the vision that itself gives us. The completed idea of it is incomprehensible without that of Revelation, and so of the Self-Revealer, and *vice versâ*. It is a direct relation to That to which it responds, and is not even itself coherent so long as its Object is denied. And with that paradox—if such it be—we leave this main division of our subject (but for the appended note), only awaiting such completion as it shall find in the treatment of those other ideas with which it is inseparably involved.

NOTE TO CHAPTERS III AND IV

Unwilling as we are unduly to elaborate our subject, there is one aspect of the Theory of Knowledge which so closely concerns the general argument of the two preceding chapters—and, in one way or another, much that will follow—that we venture to devote to it the parenthetical attention of a note.

The common component of both reason and the explicit Revelation we are assuming is the proposition or judgement symbolized by the formula "S is P". In thinking, we call it a judgement: in communication, a proposition. Now, if it can be shown that the function of the proposition is the primary: that its meaning is the more coherent and rational: that it, and not the other, relates to man in his concrete reality as a unitary individual: then we shall understand Revelation—which is God's communication—better, and how and why it transcends and transforms the intellectual situation as a whole. Let us look into this.

A judgement, or opinion, is not, yet is expressed in, a proposition. Now a proposition is an answer to a question, or at any rate the imparting of information as from one who knows it to one who does not. But, when I form an opinion, I am both questioner and answerer, or the one who is ignorant and the one who knows. It may be said, indeed, that the questioner *becomes* the answerer: that there is no anomaly in simply propounding a question to oneself. But in fact the formula of judgement implies that I am both simultaneously. The questioner must survive for the answerer to answer him. Now this latent irrationalism becomes explicit when we come to first principles. However modest I may be, I cannot help regarding myself—that is, myself *quâ* answerer—as the holder of the key that fits the lock. If I do not somehow assume that, then I simply admit my personal incompetence to think out the question, and the problem is not a problem to *me* at all. With a proposition that answers another's question, it is different. In intercourse, question and answer meet from opposite directions. They are divided by the cleft that divides two personalities. There is no difficulty about this. But judgement is the meeting of question and answer—or ignorance and knowledge—within one mind. The ultimate decision is given from within. Whatever external criterion we may appeal to, first or last, we cannot escape this implication of ego-centricity. In the end this anomalous arrangement must break down. We are thrown back upon communication—the proposition. But human communication is not only unsatisfying, it is fallible. It refers us back to our own judgement, whether we judge the communication or the communicator. Judgement is a secondary and adapted form of communication. Incidentally, this seems to us very significant of the essentially social implications of personality, and of the fallacy of treating "individual" and "social" as antithetical terms. But it also indicates—and this is here the relevant point—why mere thought fails before the ultimate problems of personality and life.

But, when we come to the impact of the Eternal—or rather when it comes to us—the case is different. Faith is the act of the whole man. His relations are external. But, though he receives communication, it is not that of a finite being, who either appeals to or overrides the arbitration of his own mind. The intellect is neither ignored nor determinative. It is receptive. Confronting the Word of its Creator—then and then only—it loses its abstractness in the unity of the man.

We must believe that when, in eternity, discursive thought will no longer (as Croce puts it) "simulate communication", this will mean not only, on the one hand, the restoration of the individual as such to his true focus and freedom, but *eo ipso* the re-creation of true social life. This of course is not achieved the moment that we, as sinners, come face to face with God. But the very meaning—and fact—of faith, even prior to its triumphant issue, meets significantly the irrationalism at the heart of our reasoning processes. It helps us to see our intellectual perplexities, and pretensions also, included in a total situation which is precisely that situation which the redemptive Word and Act of the Creator goes to meet: that of a radical diremption of self from self, because also of self from its Creator. As light and life, the first endowment of our creaturehood, are one: as the Darkness and the Death are one: so the Light and Life of the New Creation are one. Thus the very meaning of the New Creation includes the initial renewal even of the very conditions under which it is known and believed. If we think of our "faculty" of judgement as something in itself intelligible and autonomous, we shall always tend to assign to the intellect a place in religious thought either too high or too low, according as we allow or merely suppress its dominance therein. But, if we see in our rational endowment, as in all else that we are, the broken image of God, we shall have glimpsed the *one* answer to the double question: "What is the call for—therefore the meaning of—His redemptive Act?" and "Why does that Act need to be articulately *revealed*?"

CHAPTER V

SCIENCE, PHILOSOPHY, AND FAITH

I

Even where it is admitted, and indeed strongly maintained, that the ultimate basis of belief is spiritual and God-given, it is commonly assumed that, within the sphere of reason, the idea of God must be *reached*. The God of reason and the God of spiritual communion are, of course, identified, but the two mental *spheres* are not brought into intelligible relation. Till this is done, only confusion and obscurity can arise. We have essayed this by approaching each from the side of the other. We have found ourselves unable to understand either reason or faith without reference to two ideas that belong, in different forms, to both: (1) in respect of the subject—self-consciousness, which becomes more and more explicit in reason and finds its climax in the self-committal of faith; (2) in respect of the object—cosmic faith, which is implicit in reason and explicit as faith in God. And, since these ideas together have answered directly and differently, *both* the question "What is reason?" and the question "What is faith?" we can claim that neither reason nor faith is to be explained *into* the other. This *mutual* reference is the completest form of unity in difference.

Keeping these conclusions in mind, we pass on, in this chapter, to the relation of Religion to other departments of thought. We shall deal particularly with one great result of the lack of a sound and definite epistemological approach, namely Rationalism. We wish to maintain, as against this tendency of thought, that religious ideas are *sui generis* and autonomous, and that the conclusions of empirical Science do not possess that kind of direct relevance to them with which they are commonly credited. We use the word "Rationalism", not in the sense of a philosophical attitude as contrasted with Empiricism as another philosophical attitude, nor yet in contrast to orthodoxy, but as the tendency to *base* belief upon inference. Our first concern, however, in this chapter, is the type of Rationalism that makes its appeal to the results of empirical enquiry.

Empiricism, whatever unwarranted claims lie behind it, is often apparently modest. It distrusts demonstrative argument and drastic theories. A cautious probabilism is all that it can aspire to. And the more contentedly if the sanctuary of faith has been found to be the true abiding-place of the soul. We need not disallow its method if we consider it as relative to the various forms of doubt and disbelief and as addressed *ad hominem.* This process need not be exhaustive, and indeed could not be, because we cannot close the door to all the questionings and objections of future times.

But, apart from its dependence at every turn upon un-detected metaphysical assumptions, its probabilism is fatal to any further claim. And not only is it not itself faith, but it stands at three removes from faith. Theology, as we shall see, though not itself faith, holds the privileged position as the primary intellectual expression of the truths revealed to faith. Religious Philosophy (epistemological and critical) holds the next place, because it brings the purely religious ideas into progressive relation with our complex and changing conceptions of life, self, and the world; also because it is its duty to understand and vindicate, on its own plane, the authenticity of faith. Philosophy *seeks* to eliminate the abstract and so to reach true concrete absolute being. This it cannot, *pace* Hegel, find within itself, but it can confess its *own* abstractness and surrender to the self-revealed Absolute. By humbling *itself* it is exalted.

Empirical Science stands at a further remove. Of this we write with diffidence. But one can and must know the frontiers of one's own area, and shape our pattern from within, relatively to contiguous areas; otherwise we should need to know everything in order to know anything. We shall endeavour to do no more.

Now Science surely occupies a far more external position than Philosophy in relation to religious ideas. In relation to these it is independent and self-contained, and the independence must be mutual. It deals with partial aspects, contingency, phenomena. Only, in fact, by some sort of alliance with Philosophy, be it only by way of illicit assumptions, can it even seem to win a right to speak—otherwise than suggestively—of ultimate things. Its principles, as has been often and justly maintained, are instruments that we use. And, though we do not doubt that its sphere is reality, and that what it finds is there, yet this does not in any way justify cross-cuts from point to point between its own universe of discourse and any other.

And thus, owing to its own chosen outlook, empirical Theism cannot even set before itself the true object of its own enquiry. The very idea of God is compromised by its method, unless the relativity of that method is steadily kept in view. For it treats God as a contingent being, that may or may not be real. And this, in itself, is not only defective but false. It does not suffice to plead that this fiction is due to the limitation of our faculties, unless we are prepared to admit that the method itself is, by virtue of this limitation, compelled to treat of God as if He were what He is not.[1]

The claims made for a philosophy of Religion based on Science—or in part based on it—draw their strength from a tendency to claim, in and for Science itself, an ideal of unity and a distinct world-view. This was easier in the confident Victorian days. But even to-day we need more caution. We need to accept definitely the limitation of the empirical horizon as such. We need to take to heart that the breaches of its continuities, the rebuffs and the revisions, are of no less positive

---

[1] This is not to be taken to imply that Empiricism is inconsistent on its own ground. It is not obliged to admit our major premiss. But this is how it appears from the standpoint of our main argument.

significance for the Theory of Knowledge than its cumulative successes. Is there any reason to expect that it will ever leave behind the liability to snags, disappointments, disillusionment? Its most advanced systemizations, surely, are no nearer to absolute system than are the rudimentary ones that it has left behind, any more than a billion is nearer to infinity than five.

It is just when we begin to distinguish consistently between the meaning and ideals of any department of mental activity within itself and its meaning *as* a department among other departments that we gain a glimpse of what a real synthesis of life and thought requires. To treat Science as if it had its own little congenital philosophical equipment, sufficient for theorizing—if not dogmatizing—about the other side of its frontier, is to live in a fool's paradise. Philosophy, no less than Religion, and even advancing Science, must continually call for revision of the simple philosophical assumptions of empirical Theism. The Empiricist may, of course, plead that we can but deal with the situation as it is at any given moment, and cannot be expected to anticipate the future: but this only shows how relative and *ad hominem* his arguments, at the bottom, must be. For laws and principles yet to be discovered are already true. Philosophy is in a far better position in this respect. For, though it revises itself even more, it is far more relative to the mental context of the particular age, and therefore—paradoxically at first sight—has a greater claim to convey to it intimations of eternal truth.

We therefore reject the familiar idea of conflict or reconciliation between Science and Religion. We agree with those who to-day are standing out for a diastasis, a sharp distinction of standpoints, corresponding to the different aspects of reality. Theology deals with the absolute, Science with the relative, including the relatively absolute. Theology deals with the sphere of real freedom, empirical Science tries at least to study the universe in its determinate aspect. Science deals with evolution, Theology with creation. Let us dwell upon this last point for a moment.

Evolution is an extraordinarily elusive and, for ultimate ontological purposes, incoherent, idea. It is useless to talk about God creating "through evolution" without defining both those words. What is evolution but the increase of organization and complexity in terms of some formula of continuity? And this implies a selected point of view. It gives to the term "evolution" a methodological significance. "Emergence", used as a term of philosophy, does not alleviate, but only veils, our perplexities. *Whence* do things emerge? If the idea of evolution can be made to include the coming into being of the really new, this only means that the chain of continuity has links—which it must have, and which we know it has. We *know* that novelties emerge.

Among the valuable features of Bergson's treatment of "Creative Evolution" is his attack on the "tout est donné" fallacy, common to Naturalists and Idealists. But both the value and the limitations of his *Évolution Créatrice* seem to us to depend upon his suspension of definite enquiry as to just *what* it is that creates and what it is that is created. The theory is balanced by the double omission. He thus clears for himself a relatively workable field. Outside that field, evolution becomes an abstract and insufficient concept. It may be regarded as an aspect of creative action, but it is also an aspect of the created world; and the consequent confusion can never be overcome till both abstractions are resolved into their respective concretes, the Creator and the creation.

It may be objected that so to hold apart evolution and creation is to forget that the world is God's world, and to make a dualistic split between nature and Deity. But we no more split them than we split a coin by looking—as we must —at each side separately. Theology and Science are at once disentangled and unified when we regard them as *aspects* of reality, instead of leaving them to quarrel, like two dogs over one bone. The unity of the universe then discloses itself, not as an adjustment, however imperfect, between the particular *conclusions* of two spheres of thought, but in the relation of these two spheres to one another.

But that is not the whole truth about that relation. We must admit that, as a matter of fact, Science does disclose features of the universe that seem to answer to the ideas of Religion—apparent teleology for instance. Without these there could not even seem to be discrepancy or reconciliation. And certainly objection would rightly be raised if we treated this fact as meaningless for the religious mind as such. We may justly be asked to bring the fact of this correspondence into relation with the general view that we have advanced. This claim will be met by our claim for the idea of God itself, that it is behind all other ideas. It is their completion because it is their bedrock.

Take for instance such ideas as those of energy and causation. From our point of view, had we space to dwell upon this, they would appear as abstractions from the personal concepts— will, purpose, and desire; and will itself as only fully comprehensible in the light of the absolute creativity of God. So again with necessity and chance. Now Science uses these secondary concepts. The business of theistic philosophy is, not to draw inferences from them, but to exhibit, in the light of its own datum, their inherent instability and abstractness. The great point upon which we have to insist is this: that, having once undertaken *at the start* to approach the whole subject from the side of plenary Divine Being—however vaguely conceived at the beginning—these abstractions come to be seen as what they are. It is no matter of inference. The only reserve to be made concerns the entire point of view, which needs to verify itself in the end, proximately to reason, finally to faith.

From our point of view, therefore, the quasi-Divine features (if we may use the term) of nature are not so much proofs as glimpses of God. As God is behind nature, so our idea of God is behind our ideas of nature. This does not involve any crude and obsolete theory of "innate ideas", as if the idea of

God pre-existed in us in a realistic non-psychological sense. Rather that we, minds and all, exist in it: that it is creative of our own minds *pari passu* with the universe, material and mental, to which we belong. For it is not "It". The true idea of God is not passive and detachable from the reality: it is one with Himself, the self-communicating Life and Light.

But this subjective help that Science gives to so many minds—both in thinking out and in more vitally enjoying the higher truths—constantly tends to be taken as rational evidence, liable, therefore, to be paid for in rational doubt. And the more so as we are often obliged to use compromising terms, physical and anthropomorphic, to express our idea of God, which give that colour of contingency, already noticed, that renders it, at the cost of impaired truth, an object that empirical methods can handle.

Consequently, if we must think of God in terms of His positive relation to nature, so we must also think of Him in terms of detachment and unlikeness. And we cannot say beforehand how much of the one and how much of the other we are to have. Thus while all analogies, intimations, "explanations" offered by Science tend to keep alive our sense of the reality of God, the same applies, in another and complementary sense, to every flaw upon the mirror, every breach of correspondence, every snag that we encounter in the visualization of the Unseen. For these offer, each in its own way, release from the dominance of the relative. These things are, as difficulties, properly only subjective—failures of too ambitious imagination, impotencies of thought, uneasy breathing in the rarefied atmosphere of the lonely mountain-top. But they feed our sense of that *mysterium tremendum* which is itself an element in the experience of the Divine. For God as transcendent is simply "God" as noun, not as adjective; and this transcendence is not mere immensity, merely the rejection of compromising symbolism, imperfect embodiments, well-meant idolatries, but paradox. It will be remembered that Otto calls attention to the glorification of

God's wisdom and greatness, in the book of Job, evoked by the apparent *failures* of meaning and teleology in the behaviour of certain animals.

Some familiarity with this general point of view, in an incomplete form, is common enough. We are now ready to admit that Science cannot tell us about absolute origins. Let us only carry through this mental revolution. Wherever any religious doctrine is said to conflict with a scientific conclusion, we can always set on the one side what it is that Science pure and simple really says, and on the other what it is that Theology, clarified and concentrated, retains as its inherent right. Intellectually, the theological doctrine may seem then fine-spun, and elusive to our familiar modes of thinking; but it will be really, in the end, more concrete, more immediately and simply the expression of faith, more severely relevant to the central meaning of the Gospel.

Nature is a mirror of God, a mirror at once circumscribed, dimmed, and broken. And this includes, not merely the artistic and *primâ facie* aspects of nature, but all that Science teaches or can teach, nay even our minds that teach and are taught it. We are still too apt to regard it as crassly objective and "governed" by laws. To object against things alleged by Christianity that they are "contrary to experience", or even to admit that they require more evidence because they are rare, is false induction. Whether or no we are inclined to defend the old view of miracles, we ought never to allow such a fallacy to pass. Even in respect of the supernormal (apart from any particular theory about it), this attitude of scepticism is, in the same way, unjustified. Infrequency is not a valid objection, unless there is reason to believe that the alleged happenings would occur frequently if at all. And Christianity is by hypothesis unique, unrepeatable, invasive. True, it is also, by its meaning, related through and through to all life and all knowledge. But to these as a whole and as such, not directly in respect of special ideas, discoveries, or laws.

The matter has been approached from the other side, in order to show that Science owes its root principles to Christian Theism. But let it suffice to try—as we have tried—to understand the abiding relation between the two as it affects our religious thought. We may perhaps usefully sum it up as follows: (1) Science extends indefinitely our visualization of the material universe which God transcends; and this transcendence is significant just because the universe contains within itself intimations of some of those Divine qualities which, in God, transcend it. (2) By virtue of the "difficulties" it raises, religious thought is forced to understand and assert its own supremacy, and to concentrate on the really relevant. (3) The study of the scientific *method* must surely throw new light upon the Theory of Knowledge—therefore of religious knowledge—in respect of the interaction of the different departments of mental activity.

II

What has been said about Science applies *mutatis mutandis* to the Science of Mind. But the latter has peculiar interest. The New Psychology has made us familiar with certain mental processes which run closely parallel with spiritual acts and experiences, for instance, auto-suggestion on the one hand and prayer on the other. There are two ways of meeting such cases which are both wrong. We may explain away the spiritual explanations into them, whether with sceptical or with apologetic intent. Or we may dodge them, and welcome with pleasure anything which seems to discredit what the investigators have asserted. The latter, besides the lack of intellectual candour, stakes the stability of spiritual ideas on the chance of alleged discoveries not being true—a chance which extends beyond the present situation to an indefinite future. The former is Rationalism, positive or negative. We are not here concerned with its direct denials, but with the tendency to subject religious to humanly discovered truth, whether this takes the form of "liberal" reconstruction of religious doctrines or of misgiving for the safety of the historic faith.

The problem may thus be formulated. We first set side by side e.g. the phenomena of auto-suggestion with the occurrence of answers, or apparent answers, to prayer, so far as prayer relates to the condition, mental or physical, of the person who prays. Now if we keep the two sets of phenomena apart, their resemblance confronts us as something to be explained. But all empirical explanations start from the demand to minimize fortuitous coincidences. The impulse therefore—and it is a right impulse—is to bring them together into one.

This may be done in either of two ways. We may subsume prayer under auto-suggestion—that is, affirm that it is nothing but auto-suggestion—whether in support of pure Naturalism or of some form of non-supernatural religion. This, however, virtually begs the whole question of the general validity of the naturalistic method. It is no argument against supernaturalism, unless it be the case that no other method of joining the two sets of phenomena is possible.

The other way is to treat auto-suggestion as a rudimentary form of part of what prayer is. If we approach it from this side, the difficulty disappears. If we thus lose something of the direct evidential value of successful prayer as a unique phenomenon, we can well afford to let this go. Our faith, even intellectually, rests upon deeper foundations.

That auto-suggestion is imperfect prayer is the view of Dr William Brown, and we think it is on the right lines. He has remarked a tendency in patients to advance spontaneously from mere belief in the efficacy of this curative method to a sense that "the universe is friendly". Here we seem to see auto-suggestion self-interpreting in the light of that which is not itself. But even if this end is realized so far as may be, this is not the ultimate resting-place. For the Ultimate is not merely ultimate: it is the Alpha as well as the Omega. We end with it to begin afresh, till Time is gathered up into Eternity. The automatic universe cannot be friendly, only God.

And so, in our thinking about ultimate truth, continuity always finds discontinuity beyond it. It is just this broken and arrested unity of nature within and without us, calling for a fulfilment that it has not in itself, that makes this coherence with religious ideas possible, and saves the religious mind from a position of isolation without compromising its supremacy. Neither likeness alone nor contrast alone could satisfy this requirement of thought.

And when we come to inspect the logical coherence of the auto-suggestive method in itself, we find it imperfect. There is a discrepancy in its meaning regarded from without and regarded from within. To produce changes in ourselves by affirming inwardly that they are already there is as theoretically incoherent as it is practically effective, like the opening of an exhibition by declaring it open. And the idea of the action of self upon self discloses more and more its relative and provisional character as auto-suggestion penetrates to the organic centre, where we know ourselves as units of action and suffering. Real transformation is from without. Behind the mechanism of process appears dimly the "friendly universe", only waiting to receive its own final meaning in the revelation of the redeeming God.

And so we might go on to other things. There is the well-known psycho-analytic bugbear "wish-fulfilment"; in particular the explanation of belief in God by self-projection, due to the desire for an ideal Alter Ego. But this argument against the reality of God applies only if we sustain our belief by reliance on the *fact* of our belief. We have no need to dispute aught that is positive in this theory. We have only to see the lower drawn into the orbit of the higher. God *is*, in the fullest sense that answers to the craving in the unconscious, the Alter Ego of each of us. And that this Alter Ego should be the Creator, and so be at once the fulfilment of ourselves and the "Wholly Other" is a paradox that, from the higher plane, rationalizes the psychological paradox of the lower. Let us consider this for a moment longer.

By hypothesis the Creator is His creature's Alter *Ego* (in the fullest sense of the demand) because the very meaning of creatural existence is rooted in the will and essence of the Creator, with whose moral nature—barring later deflections—his own is literally one. By hypothesis too he is individually other than his Creator—a point that we are apt to blur by explanations of creation as the "thoughts of God". For existence is *given* to him, and he is an object—not introspectively—to God. Thus the oneness of our ideal nature with God and the personal otherness are two sides of the same truth. We can set the coherence of the creationist explanation against the incoherence of self-projection, considered in itself and by itself.

We can, of course, as in the former case, leave the incoherence where it was. But it may be asked whether even an unconscious process could spring from an entirely illogical root. Logic, at the bottom, is the actually thinkable, not merely what we ought to think. At any rate, though the fragment of an idea may not seem a fragment to those who find it only in our disordered souls, this need not trouble any who accept the whole into which it fits. That this is enough to say here is obvious, if we steadily bear in mind the purpose of this essay, not to adduce empirical evidence for Theism, but to exhibit its inclusive rationality on the supposition of its truth. (The success of this attempt would be, as a fact in itself, empirical evidence.)

III

Before leaving this part of the subject, there is one very widely used conception that underlies empirical and other forms of Theism, and demands some attention; namely, that of Immanence. Is it correct to assume that, if God has created the universe, He must be *in* all that is good in its elements and processes, and especially in the main advance of evolution? (We defer for the present any question of a "Fall".)

Brunner, as a Barthian, denies the immanence of God in an epistemological sense; that is, that we *know* God in the universe; but he regards it as obviously true that He *is* in the universe, though how, we do not know. But there does not seem to be much meaning in the assertion that God is—objectively—immanent, but not self-revealed to us as such. At best the idea rests upon a physical metaphor, and if it conveys no intimation to our minds as to why, how, or in what sense, that metaphor is applicable, it has no claim to be regarded as true.

The counter-principle to that of immanence is, of course, transcendence. Now if we glance briefly at the mutual relation of these two terms, we observe that they seem to approach one another, but with a difference.

Beginning with immanence, and minimizing the alloy of physical metaphor (impersonality, diffusion, indirect action), we arrive at the idea of a Supreme Being at the centre of all things, who from that centre controls the finite centres, and is the source, for the finite individual, of all life, thought, and aspiration, so far as these express the true meaning of his existence and destiny. This is only a rough indication, and may be completed and revised at pleasure. But it suffices to show how immanence passes into transcendence. Indeed, we are insensibly led to invert the idea, so that it takes the old form summarized by St Paul: "In Him we live and move and have our being"—the world immanent in God. For, as we think out the universality and unity of His presence, it no longer is contained but contains: as we think out its depth, it is no longer within but beneath: as we think out its activity, we find creativeness, and, if creativeness, otherness. "Immanence" is overcharged and collapses from within.

"Immanence" has relative and controversial truth. It served for the Darwinian sceptic and others, but it is a deceptive instrument of constructive thought. As long as we said "*God* is in nature"—as against naturalistic Evolutionism—we were mainly right. When we say "God is *in* nature"—as a religious philosophy—we have pressed into our service a metaphor that we cannot control.

But now let us scrutinize transcendence. What is it that God transcends? Not surely a neutral and irrelevant universe, not a humanity created in an alien image, not mere apparent values that this same transcendence disallows. It is little to enthrone God above a scrap-heap. The last word of the doctrine of transcendence is that God transcends even the highest, even the adjectivally divine, even the immanence of His own attributes. It is the transcendence of the *glory* of man that is the glory of God, of the barrier of distance that makes Him near, of Man that makes Him the Saviour of men. All that is true in immanence may be stated in terms of transcendence.

(But we have yet to consider the relation of God to man as affected by sin. Till then we have not seen all the pitfalls of Immanentalism.)

IV

We are devoting no long section to the relation of Philosophy to religious knowledge. Our answer to this question, already anticipated in the present chapter, runs through the book, and is illustrated by its own method. But we may here appropriately sum up our general view of this relation.

(1) Philosophy is not the completest and most concrete form of truth. It is *within* life, and a *department* of thought.

It cannot reach the Concrete by its own efforts, for the very reason that it is itself differentiated from ordinary life and thought by an act of abstraction. Neither abstract Being nor a typical object analysed into sensations will set us going on the right road. That is the first essential to understand.

(2) But life itself, for most of us, does not reach its own true concreteness, and never fully possesses it. That goal, by our hypothesis, is to be realized in God.

(3) However, Philosophy is not an outsider. But the Concrete must be *given to* it. God must be self-revealed to the philosopher; and that not merely in the sense that, having found Him, he must perceive that the finding is due to the faculties and light that He has given to him, but articulately at the start.

(4) The philosopher, in surrendering himself to the Revealer, surrenders the philosophical reflection which is part of himself. This becomes the channel, perhaps the chief channel, through which the revelation is carried on. That God's Revelation accepts a pre-adapted channel—however needing repair—rests on the truth that his Revealer is also his Creator.

(5) The function of Philosophy, radically regarded, is to remove, by the new light given it, the false ideas and assumptions, deeply rooted in our minds, that inhibit the apprehension of the highest truth. And this includes, not merely conscious theories, but much that underlies even what we are accustomed to regard as common-sense thinking. Religious thought, thus clarified and disentangled, will draw itself together round that centre in us which is the true focus, not only of the intellect, but of will and desire.

Thus the idea of God claims to rule Philosophy (from however far back), but not to rule Science. The mutual interaction of philosophical ideas with direct faith must not be confused with the subjective, non-rational alternation of the stoking with the glow, which is all that Empiricism can give. The ideal of the former is progressive annexation: the latter lives in the rhythm of detachment and assimilation, of paradox and illustration, of contrast and parallel. The seeker after a sign, in the material world, has no sign given him. But to the seeker after wisdom, the very thing he seeks *is* given; for the message is the wisdom of God.

V

This may be a suitable place for the consideration of a point which must be on no account passed over, if we are to clinch our main argument. What is the relation of faith to the sacred history? It is only necessary to fix our attention on the minimum which, it might seem, even a very thoroughgoing critic will wish to secure if he is to accept Christianity as a Divine entrance into history. (And that so it is we have taken as its primary truth-claim.) For even one who would let the whole Resurrection narrative go would be likely to stand out for so much at least of the record of Christ's life and teaching as will either (according to his mode of approach) set us upon the road to an experience of His Divine "value" or not contradict the faith and doctrine of the Church about His Personal Redemptive Work.

What is the attitude that ought to be taken by those who believe that Christianity is at once historical—at least at a minimal point—and yet *absolutely* verifiable to the spirit of man? Let us in no way evade the stringency of the issue. We may reduce the historical residuum to the very minutest, but still the Revelation does not complete its circle round the soul. The quality of probabilism remains. Whatever provisional value empirical considerations may have in cutting off the attacks of doubt which our faith is insufficient to withstand, a faith that tries to *incorporate* them is not faith but opinion. Faith can absorb Philosophy, for Philosophy may seek the absolute, but historical evidence remains unassimilated, an external aid. The empirical is indeed, in another sense, always present to faith; the biographical *fact* that God has given to us in our personal lives what He has given, and has shown to us what He has shown: but this evidence is self-evidence: the content of the Revelation is the verification of the fact of it. This is not empirical *inference*.

But this biographical fact is found to be continuous with a wider fact, the solidarity of our spiritual knowledge with that of a community and with a historical tradition. We know when and in whose Person—or in the belief in whose Person—both started. If therefore the personal experience does not rest on the historic record, yet at least the minimal essence of that record—wherever we may fix it—finds a credential in the experience. But is the converse true? That is our crucial question.

The weight of our souls rests on the unseen Presence, the inwardly spoken Word. We cannot therefore say that experience and history support one another on equal terms. Relatively speaking, no doubt, the history is a verification of the experience, but only in so far as the experience as a fact is used as evidence, not when and in so far as it is in living operation. In the long last, what we have from Christ we have, what we hear from Him we hear; and no historical conclusions can invade this sanctuary or shake its ultimate foundations. If *per impossibile* what is present to us now is not connected with, and does not illuminate, a Divine Event visible in the character and teaching, in the work and sufferings, of One identifiable with the historic Jesus, the self-evidence of the redeeming God remains. Incredible conclusions follow, but so much the worse for the hypothesis that leads to them. Nothing can invalidate *ex post facto* the witness of the Spirit.

CHAPTER VI

ETHICS, THEOLOGY, AND FAITH

Kant, as is well known, attempted to secure the autonomy and absoluteness of the moral imperative by refusing to explain it in terms of values, or the positive *content* of the various duties. Conscience, though of course it refers us to particulars, does not owe its authority to any of these, not even to any one of them that may be central and supreme. Our duty is to obey duty, and so *ad infinitum*. The problem that Kant had before him has never lost its urgency, and is, as we shall try to indicate, only the theoretical side of the total situation. Duty is at once essentially absolute and essentially concrete and empirical; but it is not fully realized as both in our experience. At the same time the fact that it is not is contrary to its inherent meaning. The modern breakdown of the traditional standards, the weakening appeal of those relatively absolute values that have shored up thought and life, brings the terms of this antinomy now face to face.

Troeltsch, who, at least in his later days, was strongly impressed with the pervading uncertainty and relativity of human thought, referring to the recognized demands of conscience as "the general formal standards which proceed from the nature of the Moral Consciousness", says of them nevertheless: "We shall not be able, like the most severe of modern ethical thinkers, to deduce them simply from the universality and objectivity of the moral reason, or only and immediately from the conception of a categorical imperative. We shall have to consider that Ethics is an action; and that all action is the realization of ends; and therefore that the unity of Ethics too can only be deduced from the end, as indeed even Kant finally realized in some of his incidental and auxiliary thinking."[1] Troeltsch's conclusion upon the whole matter is that Ethics is *necessarily* beset with this uncertainty and conflict, and that even Christianity is "in the long run a tremendous continuous compromise between the Utopian demands of the Kingdom of God and the permanent conditions of our actual human life". By this is not meant, of course, the crude compromise between duty and inclination that could not be defended without direct self-contradiction. But human life itself is "primarily a struggle between the life of nature and the life of the Spirit that rises above nature and yet remains bound to nature, even whilst it turns against it".[2]

So far as Ethics is concerned with value, it is undoubtedly true that, as he says, conflict, change, and mutual adjustment belong to the essence of the human situation. And conscience itself, the imperative, is implicated in the special claims of values, just because they *are* claims, and sways with them. We know that the very distinction between right and wrong is often challenged. But the last abattis across our path is this: that Kant, if he was wrong, was also right: that the imperative of conscience is by its meaning always and everywhere absolute, therefore both lucid and practicable; and yet—look around and within.

An attempt will be made in this chapter to exhibit, in one of the various possible ways, the nature of the final *impasse*, and to show how its solution comes to us only from the dimension of faith.

I

The problem, then, is essentially practical. And, as we hope it will be seen, the disclosure of the "irrationalism" that infects the *idea* of the moral imperative is *ipso facto* the diagnosis of its weakness in action. Lofty appeal cannot make Ethics a religion, any more than religion becomes truly ethical by translating it into the ethical categories. The

[1] *Christian Thought*, p. 50.
[2] *Op. cit.* pp. 165, 166.

antithesis of Law and Grace is the key to the fulfilment of the one in the other. The mind cannot hold to the unity of what is not first sharply distinguished. There is no true correlation between an emotional moralism and a Pelagian Gospel.

The line that we propose to take is that of the relation of the eternal moral law to the time-process as such. The special antithesis that we have before us is that of freedom and moral impotence.

Man's inability of himself to do right, even though we regard this inability as only partial, is a simple fact, a datum. We cannot eliminate the ideas of hindrance and of effort, and therefore of possible failure. We cannot explain them exclusively in terms of the resistant *material*—whether our physical organism or our environment—upon which we have to work. For nothing could possibly resist the moral will as such were there not indeterminacy and possible defeat within itself. A hindrance to a perfectly good and persistent intention would be merely external, practical, and non-moral.

And yet, for all that, the internal impotence of the moral will is, in the end, unthinkable. We cannot bring together the ideas of impotence and of responsibility. In truth, though we speak of "strength of will", the will, as we have seen, is not, in itself, properly a power, but decision. Failure, so far as it is really *failure*, belongs to our sinfulness, but not to our sins. It is not transgression.

And choice implies full consciousness of the issue. But this *full* consciousness would turn all our sins into sheer moral apostasy. Yet we habitually think of sins—not merely of moral delinquencies—as a matter of degree. And this is perfectly right within the sphere of practical relativity. Most certainly we are not to quarrel with the conceptions that day by day work the machinery of our moral life, individual and social. But they fail us when, in the interest of the higher spiritual life—or even of a grounded and reflective morality—we try to understand the meaning of Sin as such. We are not then dealing with Ethical Theory simply within itself, but in respect of its basis—a question that we cannot avoid even by declaring that it is its own basis.

Sin is at once "lawlessness" and a paradoxical impotence that abandons us into the hands of that lawlessness. And the very crux of the matter is this: that these two ideas not only remain more or less abstract and fail to find adequate illustration in the concrete world-life to which nevertheless they essentially refer us, but are apparently incompatible with one another. The mere fact of this imperfect exemplification does not annul the incompatibility. It is one side of the same fact.

Let us approach the heart of the problem by asking a question that will lead us directly into it: "Is the act of obedience separable from the intention, or not? Are they two facts or one?"

We answer first: they are one. For the act is virtually performed *in* the intention, and, if the intention needs renewing, the act, so regarded, is renewed in it; and then the intention, and so the act, has been imperfect *as such*. Or external opportunity to "strike while the iron is hot" may intervene and save us from our own weakness. Then obviously the intention is one with the act.

But also we must answer: they are two. For mere spontaneity is not obedience. It is above or below it. Decision is of the essence of obedience, and decision is decision *to* act. It may take an appreciable time. We often, and rightly, speak of obedience to duty when it is a matter of fixed habit or of moral principle in full automatic working. But that does not touch the fundamental question. The real nature of duty appears—so far as it appears at all—when it is faced by a more or less effective counter-appeal. Even the man who has been good and conscientious from infancy would not know the meaning of duty—therefore could not strictly be conscientious—if he did not think of it in that way. And deciding is a mental process. The timeless act is its abstract ideal. It may cover a second or many years. And though, of course, the act also takes time, it takes a different time. The decision *passes into* it.

The ideal of the moral life—the actually operative ideal, if we are serious at all—starts from the separateness of the intention and the act, and aims at their fusion. Hence the call, sometimes wise, sometimes feverish and impatient, to *act*, not merely to will. The motto "Do the next thing" is eminently sound when there *is* a new thing requiring new decision. It really does approximate to the true solution, but ever only approximates. And in this lies the difficulty, theoretical and practical. And, as the field of duty is the time-sphere, so its incoherences, in relation to that sphere, darken our consciences and dislocate our lives.

On the one hand, duty is direct and absolute. Where impossible, it is no longer duty: where difficult, the duty is to try: where even that is difficult—for it may be—the same applies, and so *ad infinitum*. On the other hand, impotence, partial at least, is a *fact* of the moral life, which may change its form and direction, but which no theoretical re-interpretation can remove.

And now we see how Time enters as an irreducible aspect of an "irrationalism" that splits the very idea of duty in twain. There can be no intention—that is, deliberate act—without a time-interval between the felt demand and the compliance. For, otherwise, there would be spontaneity, which, though it might express moral qualities, would not be, in any relevant sense, a moral act. And yet, on the other hand, there can be no time-interval, for the will is direct and immediate. When we will anything that we *cannot* at once carry out, the action, when the time comes, either requires a new act of the will or has already been effected, by anticipatory imagination, in the former act.

"When I would do good, evil is present with me." Present to insert itself between the intention and the act, as the fact of temporality enables it to do. When temptation is literally and absolutely sudden, then the fall it occasions is simply part and parcel of a sinful state, not a sin *per se*. All actual sin—that is, new sin—means that the will of the time—be it a year, an hour, or an instant—is not the will that made or kept the good intention. We strain to bridge the gulf in advance: we try to make the good intention a virtual anticipation of the act or acts: we secure it by every medicament we know to resist the poisonous atmosphere of our life-journey: we wish that we could telescope our future together and dispose of it as, at our best, we would. But, when we would do good, life, for all its ideals, remains ununified; and, when we would understand, thought, however practical, remains abstract.

From two different angles, complementary yet never quite convergent, we seek to overcome the discrepancy between volition and action, to rejoin what God has joined together. They answer respectively to the two post-Communion prayers in the Anglican liturgy. Either, recurrently, we present our bodies a living sacrifice—gather up life as a whole in advance, so as to pre-enact, so far as may be, the future in the present—or we seek to break up life into indivisible units, so that, act by act, as occasion comes, we may do all those good works that God has prepared for us to walk in.

But, unfortunately, the very structure of the present, as it appears in our actual time-system, sets a limit to both, even both together. Present time, so regarded, eludes the absolute punctual present, which is at once the point at which eternity inserts itself and the focus of human volition. It is never realized, either in the would-be inclusive act of self-consecration or in the ideally unbroken chain of faithfulness moment by moment. It is infected by irrationalism, theoretical and practical. When we would do good, still, in the gap between the purpose and the deed, evil is present with us.

Duty, when we try to bring it into focus, spreads over life as a whole or contracts into indivisible points. And this elusiveness is made critical by the fact that to be elusive is contrary to the idea of duty.

Duty is a path that we all must tread; but it is a blind alley till the gate that confronts us is unlocked from the other side. Troeltsch, as he accepts the fundamental necessity, in this world, of conflict and compromise, so also sees that the solution is religious. "It is not for nothing that religion, which everywhere transcends all morality, teaches us that the pure will and devotion to an ideal world is sufficient for righteousness, and that life itself remains sinful—a mixture, that is to say, of nature and the divine life. Justification by faith is only a specifically religious expression for this universal relation of things." But we are still in the morass of irrationalism if the subject-matter of faith is not factually and specifically real. And this assurance can only come from a new dimension. But there is another ethical problem, of which the same may be said, that of the source—or the seat—of the imperative.

II

We are all familiar with the argument for Theism drawn from the moral imperative. Moral obligation implies obligation to a personal Being, and our thought of this Being must be adequate to this supreme relation which He bears to ourselves. But it is not mere empirical argument that concerns us, as though we held the two ideas as external to one another, and *argued from* the law to the Lawgiver. Rather we should call attention to the *immanence* of the idea of the Lawgiver in that of the law, to the instability of the very concept of the imperative if we try to isolate it, even provisionally. As soon as we rise above the bare idea of taboo, as soon as we moralize (as we must moralize) obligation, the implication of personal relationship is there. It may find an outlet in mythology, in metaphor, in some sort of unconscious personalizing of the law itself or of conscience: it sheds all but its last irrationalism on the highest peaks of Old Testament religion. But, in any case, the demand, being a demand, is from without. It speaks within, but not *from* within. If we try to soften our idea of it, if we express it in terms of our better self, we have not gone far enough back. It is not self's law to self, not Duty's *appeal* to us: it is external and it is imperative. And thus, until God is more than Lawgiver, the old theoretical embarrassments —which are also practical—remain. But we can approach a little nearer yet to the furthest reach of Ethical Theory, where it awaits, in helpless bankruptcy, the new dimension.

Regarded in relation to the imperative, there are three types of duty:

First, there is bare command, which does not also *appeal* to anything in us, but simply says "You must". Here, however we may wish to exclude it, the implication of warning and penalty is essential. Of course, if we press this to an extreme, we can see that a moral demand that does not in any way *appeal* to the moral nature does not really reach us as a *moral* demand at all. But the approximations to it, where this appeal is heard only as an undertone, are extremely familiar. And this discloses a curious anomaly. For, while it is the most superficial form that duty can assume, and is only available for the mere police functions of morality, it yet possesses one feature essential to the fullest and deepest moral claim: namely that it presupposes no asset in us. In this respect it represents the whole scope of the Divine Law; and, if it seems to compromise, that is only because it is silent where it is useless to speak.

Secondly, there is the call of *ideals*, which all serious persons recognize to be no mere invitations for free acceptance or innocent rejection. But here it is the demand that is in the background, the appeal that is to the fore. The call of an ideal is essentially the call to make the ideal one's own: it is a call for spontaneity, and therefore an appeal to spontaneity. Every appeal *for* right motive is also an appeal *to* it, whether the germ is really there, in the given case, or not. Therefore, just because it does presuppose some asset in us, this likewise cannot have full play.

Take, for instance, the Greek and the modern conception

of a lie. It has been regarded as a point in favour of the Greek word ψεῦδος that it gives a wider content and a deeper meaning to truthfulness, by its fuller connotation of the opposite, as against the rigid taboo arbitrarily limited to a definite lie. This may be true, but, on the other hand, by this very fact, it blunts the edge of the imperative by making it vaguer and more exacting. We cannot have it both ways.

Thirdly, there is a type or aspect of duty which holds together, however imperfectly, the other two, and marks the furthest point of Ethics, where it awaits the coherence that only Revelation can give it. And it is just because we want to understand the relation of Revelation to human ideas and terminology where their *fullest* resources are exhausted that we desire to be clear about this third point. It is this: the claim of *moral goodness as a whole* on behalf of itself, not of this or that act or thought because of its particular goodness: the call to accept, and loyally follow, virtue—its duties and ideals—in place of any lower attraction that may rival it. We cannot always separate, in the actual facts, this third claim from the other two. They overlap and merge in many different ways. It is present implicitly in every moral decision that is not a mere judgement about relevant facts. But it is the deepest moral issue, and claims to be met face to face. It is the claim of *Goodness as such*, the call, not of particular ideals, but to honour all ideals. It is the essence of all ideals, the imperative behind all imperatives. And it is a *necessity* of ethical thought.

Without this distinction—very much overlooked—we cannot understand the ethical side of religion or the meaning of spiritual freedom. If this claim of the Good in itself can be presented in black and white, and under transformed mental conditions, then there is a clear issue before the human will, the call to a moral *relation* which is the basis of all moral practice. But, if not, there is a worse gap than ever. The Good personified, but not a person, is broken up among a thousand goods, or a phantom remote from them all. And God as an hypothesis can only be a helpful *thought*, not the concrete solution of a concrete situation. Such a solution can only come from another dimension, from a sphere that takes in the entire deadlock. And this means that the Law itself, while still in authority on its own plane, is transcended. Only God could have solved the problem in act before it was solved in theory. Only God could break the continuity of human dialectic and restore it from without.

III

Theology, to which we now turn, has been described in the previous chapter as holding a privileged position as the primary intellectual expression of the truths revealed to faith. The fact that even it uses human words and concepts must not blind us to its supreme and autonomous rights. We have previously urged that, in Theology as such, concepts, not words only, are simply instrumental. They too must be taken up and laid down according as they assist our vision and our communication. We should be saved from much embarrassment if we would recognize this more consistently. Not only should we be freer from their dominance, but we should be freer to exercise our own rightful dominance over them. We should not baldly contradict, for instance, terms that suggest wrong ideas about God without careful "phenomenological" scrutiny of their true inwardness. We should find substitutes if we could. We should darn rather than draw together, or even leave the hole. If no satisfactory term were forthcoming, we should remember that God's truth is not responsible for the inadequacy of our language, and that we must set right our own mental confusion as best we can. The refusal, as well as the use, of a particular form of expression may be due to our slavery to words.

And Theology must not be ashamed of its own vocabulary, as it is apt to be to-day. Its special terms are not mere moulds

—albeit necessary moulds—in which spiritual truths are confined, cooled, and hardened. If they are judiciously used, they are vitalized by those spiritual intuitions whose needs they serve. The intuition grows through its expression, and cannot be analysed out from it. And the more the term is *appropriated* by Theology, the more plastic, not the more rigid, should it become. It is partly for this reason that we do not need continually to change such terms. And the very fact that a given term of Theology—whether mainly its own or adapted—stands in relative isolation from the current thoughts of men makes it a more serviceable instrument to the religious mind. No doubt we have often to translate this language into the accustomed forms. Informal theology, if free from irreverent familiarities, has its own place. But Theology must be allowed to speak its own language too, even if men have to learn it. It must, like Science and Philosophy, mould its own vocabulary.

That theological ideas do not fit *into* our rational framework follows from all that we have said: and we shall have occasion to illustrate this later, when we come to the content of the Christian Gospel. But this is not to admit that they are, in any but the technical sense, irrational. Direct indication of super-rational truths is their primary function. Their responsibilities towards the general scheme outside Theology come after.

But not so in respect of their mutual logical implications *within* Theology. Here they *must* hold together. If we have not reached the ultimate synopsis, there must be at least coherence, not merely harmony. Unsystematic theology may be only sloppy thinking. Theology must first be true to itself, before its interplay with Philosophy. Its logical unity and its unity as a spiritual whole within experience are not different unities, but different aspects of the same. Rational intuition must always *tend* to coalesce with spiritual, though in this life always imperfectly.

Religious faith, as we have seen, gathers up into itself the comprehensive cosmic faith which is the background of belief and the presupposition of all reasoning; and, in so doing, its object becomes God, self-revealing. And this self-revelation, as we shall maintain, becomes finally explicit in the Gospel of Redemption. Faith deals with totalities, on the subject-side and on the object-side. On the one hand, it is the action of the *whole* man. On the other, it is directed towards all reality as centred in God. *Theology is monolithic.* A plurality of doctrines, fundamentally separable, belongs to the natural order. Faith, as a single focused totality-act, can see but one luminous point, and all else in its light. What that point is we shall presently enquire of Theology itself.

A glance at the relation of Theology to the Bible will conclude our chapter. The revival of the appeal to the written Word is a great feature of the Barthian movement, and not of that alone. This appeal was very much called for. If the Christian Revelation is genuinely an utterance, as well as an act, from Eternity into Time, the Bible, as its *de facto* vehicle, is necessarily, in some distinctive sense, our *de jure* authority. And, if the Christian message is taken—as we shall take it— intensively, or focally, there need be no trouble about the claims of the canon as such, nor yet about critical theories. The Word is *in* the Bible, not in the strictest sense identical with it; and that not only because of human mistakes and human passions, but because, in the Bible, truth is relative to mental context. The ideas in it adhere concentrically around a circle of absolute Truth that as such is super-rational. Thus, and not as a literary structure, do the revealed truths hold together. And the more we realize this organic and logical coherence, the more does the Word of God seem, as it were, to detach itself from the literature and to live as a self-vindicating spiritual reality in the mind and soul. Not that we can ever leave the Bible behind, in this life. We must ever revert to it. But the intensive study of it, which need not always take place before its open pages, does tend to transfer the standard of belief from the words to the

Word. And the Word, once heard coherently, testifies to itself.

The biblical revelation correlates itself with the Christian mentality, corporate and individual. The individual may, of course, use corporate belief—considered apart from his own—as a means of approaching the truth. Unanimous patristic evidence of primitive belief may support, or lead us to revise, our interpretation of New Testament teaching. But this, like critical exegesis and all else, is not the final word of the Spirit. It can only have its particular degree of weight —of which we must judge for ourselves—as against other factors. Really authoritative interpretation there cannot be. It is a contradiction in terms. Such authority would supersede that which it interprets. The appeal of the Church to the Bible is the appeal to a document: the tribunal is the Spirit of God in the individual, and cannot in the nature of the case be anything else.

Of course we are here thinking only of the mature reflective individual as such. And not only so, but we reject the idea that the immature mind must be kept open for a dispassionate choice of its own religion against its maturity. If the appeal is really to the Spirit of God, He must take possession—so far as lies with us—at the earliest opportunity. To bring a child up to believe that Christianity is primarily an opinion is to give the lie to our own faith at the outset. The Truth is also the Life, and life begins before judgement is mature, if it ever is at all. And, when we add to this the spiritual and intellectual solidarity—however imperfect—of the Christian Church, we cannot overlook the corporate character of faith. The faith of the Church is the incubator of that of the individual, as it is also the sustenance of its free maturity.

CHAPTER VII

THE TRUTH OF THE IDEA OF GOD

This chapter, like the rest of the book, is not apologetic. It does not seek to prove, in the ordinary sense of proof, the truth of the idea of God. This is frankly assumed, till faith verifies it. We seek only to show the independence and coherence of faith—and so of the idea of its Object—in relation to the general claims of rationality to which our minds must submit. This indeed becomes, so soon as it is made good, a proof, deductive in one aspect, empirical in another. But such a proof is only, at the bottom, the self-surrender of our reflective thought as a "*living* sacrifice" to an already enthroned, or at least incipient, faith.

Faith and the Truth of God that meets it, these in correlation, not the latter in detachment, are our unit of discourse. But we can make the one or the other our point of departure. So we have already made faith, so now the idea of God. Whether we say that faith in its fullest meaning must be faith in God or that God can, in the long last, be apprehended only thus, is simply a matter of mode of approach.

If we have succeeded at all in making clear the rights and authority, as we understand them, that faith can claim, the foundation is laid for the type of Theism to which we are committed. We have now to ask what the primary character of that Object of belief is that confronts reason at the moment when it takes up the problem. This question, indeed, we have practically answered at an earlier stage. Even the *primâ facie* idea of God is not the minimal but the maximal, not the emptiest but the fullest. What then does it yet lack? Why is it only *primâ facie*? Not because of narrowness and thinness, but just because of its transcendent plenitude. The intellect is stunned by its infinity, and our highest concepts seem not only inadequate, but to belie it. Thus it becomes tempting to set it aside for the present, and try to work up to it from some point outside it. But no. The idea of God, faith-given, does require to be rebuilt by the minds that He has created.

The "ontological argument" for the being of God is, in general, not very popular. But we may hope that by now the genuine intellectual and spiritual urge behind the imperfect theories is coming more to light. In its Anselmic form, as M. Koyré[1] has shown, it is essentially—in spite of its formally positive character—a defence of a belief already held in possession. It is by no means an arid rationalism: its implications, in substance, though not in form, are intuitional. Its real core is this: that the idea of God—and that idea solely and uniquely—cannot be denied except it has been tampered with first. That idea lives, not by proof, but by its inherent resources. It therefore bears no burden of proof. It is on the defensive, and even the enlargements that it seems to owe to the human mind are its own recovery of its own.

But, instead of discussing this type of argument, and spending time in criticizing its several varieties, let us, having taken our start from it, leave it behind, and see whether the direction which it indicates does not lead us to a sure ground.

Let us first make constructive use of a point hitherto emphasized simply by way of avoiding misunderstanding: namely, that, throughout this book, we are assuming the idea of God as true, but true *in its own setting*; that is, as an object of corporate and individual faith, a challenge to, and a claim upon, the whole man, therefore upon the very groundwork of his thought. For those who can carry this effort through, the faith-attitude is vindicated as valid and its Object as real; and so reason, recognizing its own Creator, makes its *own* surrender to Him. Thus we may say that, in a sense, this validity and this reality are *posited* with a view to their ultimate verification.

[1] *L'idée de Dieu dans la philosophie de St Anselm.*

And yet the word "posit" is inadequate, and we must not lean our weight upon it. For faith is not the first move in an intellectual game: it is the creation of, and the response to, the revelation of God: it accepts, as we saw at the outset, not tentatively but absolutely. Subjectively, as an act, it may be weak: its object may be clouded and remote: but its "intention" goes straight to absolute Being, the "greatest conceivable". And, since it is the integral man that performs the act, or takes the attitude, this act or attitude is as truly moral and spiritual as it is cognitive: the acceptance of the will of the Object is a necessary element in the apprehension of His Being.

And all this means that the idea of God is rooted in its own soil—the new man, the new mind, the new society, the new heaven and earth that are to be. If we "posit" God, we posit all this.

Yet still how is it true to say that the idea of God, if denied, has been tampered with first? May not an Atheist have a completer and sounder idea of God—of what the word means—than many Christians? But we have never said —what would be obviously untrue—that defects in the understanding of what God is (or of the best concept that can be formed of Him, as the case may be) are the sole cause of unbelief. Everyone's idea of God is defective, and this defectiveness does not *necessitate* unbelief, but only makes it possible. The Revelation of God does not wait upon our infallibility. That is the one side of the matter. And the other is that the way to commend the truth of the Gospel is to bring home its meaning.

There are two aspects of the idea of God; and it may help us in our handling of this question if we distinguish them sharply. There is the idea as examined, analysed, tested— whether by inductive or by deductive methods—in our rational laboratory; and there is the idea considered as the inner and essential meaning of a "Wholly Other" that transcends yet confronts the entire mechanism of our minds.

The former can never do real justice to the latter, and therefore can never lay it open to refutation. The human mind has taken over the *idea* of its Creator, as a mental possession that must conform to the conditions of its adoption. And the mind does this on its own responsibility. It has no key to the unfathomable depths of the transcendent vision, which it sees, if at all, through the distorting medium of sin. Unless it lives very much in the light of this vision, it works in a dimness that not only conceals but deceives. Shaping its own conception of Deity, it cannot see how fragile are the earthen vessels which hold its treasure. Neither can it see how the imperfect thoughts which it rejects as simply errors may hold the place open for vital truths, where a gap would cause the whole structure to collapse. And again and again, the vision rises from the dead over the ashes of our thought-constructions.

We have, then, reached a point where an important distinction comes into view, the distinction between the idea of God as subjective concept and the idea as objective meaning. And the latter entirely transcends the former: there is no continuity between them. But we hasten to add that, because there is discontinuity, there is not therefore disconnection. Our private—or traditional—ideas about God have taken their start from the creation of our minds by Him. But, as with character so with thought, the old creation must pass through the new, if it is to live again. Our ideas, like our virtues, however real and vital on their own plane, must humbly take their place within that totality of the person that is but the protoplasm of the new birth. Our doubt—or more than doubt—may *de facto* inhibit the surrender of the mind and will to the Creator. The mind has no abstract right to deny the possibility of a truth that is in no way dependent on any of its arguments.

Ever the objective meaning addresses itself to the finite mind. Ever the finite thought "intends" the objective meaning. We cannot understand the one without reference to the other. But they interact from opposite directions. Underneath both, and giving them their common basis, lies the Creatorship of God. The Creator speaks to, even as He acts upon, His creation. The Light, like the Life, *intervenes*. And in it the candle-light, no less than the darkness, disappears.

That the immediacy of the Divine Truth must transform itself into the human concept is a necessity. It is part of the broad fact of the Incarnation. Our perverted intellects are not to be captured at once, and they must be met first on their own plane, and addressed in their own language. As with the personal Word, so it is with the uttered Word.

But, when reason does make its submission to God, as one side of the faith-act of personal surrender, this very act gives the key to the subjective meaning which the Divine Name bears within our own minds. Instead of shaping our subjective idea of God, and then adjusting our attitude to such a Being, we have only to establish our faith-relation with God in the first impact of His presence and unanalysed glory —even perhaps suspending all our articulate thoughts *about* Him—and *then* we find that we can think as those who know. If we look for God, we find God. If we look for the idea only, we find only the idea. And the idea, so found, is under a special disadvantage of its own. There is no universe of thought in which, like other ideas, it can take its place. For by its meaning it is prior to all; and yet we are compelled to try and fit it in. But, if we find God Himself—and, in so finding, find that He has first found us—then all the terms by which we seek to understand His nature take their place at once—personality, goodness, power, love, holiness. In the next chapter we shall have more to say about this.

It was rightly urged against the old Agnosticism that, in asserting that God could not be known, it claimed to know at least this about Him: that He could not or would not reveal Himself. The very idea of a self-revealing God, taken together with the challenge to our intellectual self-confidence that it makes, is the first breach in the encircling wall of negation, the doubt of doubt. For who can assume that the apparently strongest argument against Theism does not rest upon some hidden assumption that a flood of new light might expose and discredit, without disturbing any facts or logic upon which the argument depends, or neglecting the fundamental claims of human reason? In ordinary cases our confidence would be untouched by such a suggestion. It would be an "unmotived hypothesis". That some new light in the future should reveal to us—while accounting for all apparent evidence to the contrary—that the earth is flat would be a bolt from the blue, and to expect it as gratuitous as to expect the crash of a vast meteorite to-morrow morning. But the idea of the Revealer, as a possible reality, has no burden of proof to bear. It contradicts nothing but gratuitous negative assumptions, and no question of chances for or against enters at all. It cannot, of course, be forced upon anyone; for, by its meaning and nature, its impact is spiritual and personal. But its first whisper calls in question our intellectual situation *as a whole*, and the more urgently because it does not disturb its essential inner coherence before we can listen. That is the true super-rationality of religion.

And so we come back to the theme that we propounded at the beginning of the chapter. The case that comes before reason—so far as reason can decide it—is not, fundamentally, that of the Being of God simply, but of that and human faith in correlation. This means not only belief in God but belief in faith—its unique character, its relation to reason itself, and its claim to verification on its own ground. And this conclusion is none the less true because it is not in fact usually possible to make it a living issue, in face of intellectual bars, without the *ad hominem* employment of accepted intellectual methods.

And so we have reached by another route the main conclusions of the preceding chapters. The *primâ facie* subject-matter of reason is the idea of God as a unique spiritual and also intellectual phenomenon, truly established only in that Christian mind, corporate and spiritual, which itself has created. For, again, the idea of God, if true, *is* God, in all but its human imperfection. It does not, as we say in popular speech and in some philosophy, "correspond" to reality. It *is* the reality, self-revealing. The idea of God (here we are joining the subjective and objective aspects under one formula) is simply God Himself self-revealing through the dark and distorting medium of our own sinfulness and unbelief. As long as we look for it *in* our own minds, this does not appear. It is not a datum in that sense. Its relation to constructive thought is not that of the "spark within", but that of a double transcendence, the creative Mind behind us and the explicit evangel before. Its externality is not that of alien Being, but the otherness of the Creator. He who has made our mental world can enter it as an idea among ideas, even as He has entered the outer world as a Man among men. But that idea has no rights and no stability—even such as other ideas have within their scope—apart from His living presence. And reason, on its side, even when defensive of Theism, in the end loses all its gains if it does not point beyond itself. It cannot permanently defend the content of Revelation simply as a passive object of contemplation. It must needs confess that the Revealed *must* be the Revealer, not indirectly and immanently, but transcendently. And then it knows that God cannot be judged before He is heard, and then—that, when heard, we know His voice, and can only shut our ears or believe Him.

CHAPTER VIII

THE CONTENT OF THE IDEA OF GOD

We have tried in the previous chapter to see how the idea of God, considered as an object of faith, makes good its claim within the sphere of the intellect. In other words, we have asked, and tried to indicate, what that form of theistic philosophy is that answers to the conception of faith and reason, in their mutual involution, that we reached at the beginning. God, in the last chapter, is Anselm's "greatest conceivable", or plenary Being. This was vague, but rightly so, because we are not building up our edifice, but watching its emergence from the mist as we approach it. And now we should see it a little more clearly. We have to deal with the main features of the content of the idea of God—the "attributes of God", to use an old phrase—and to form an idea of them that will constitute a solid whole both with what precedes and with what will follow.

It is clear that, for us who seek to justify our belief in the Christian religion by way of a search for the moment of self-evidence that it contains, the answer to the question *why* we believe and the answer to the question *what* we believe must coalesce. In other words, whatever contributes to the adequacy of our idea of God contributes directly to the foundation of our belief in Him. The truth of this, indeed, broadly applied, is obvious, but it has the far greater significance for a Theism that *relies* for the stability of its belief upon the progressive understanding of the idea that claims it.

We do not forget that God is revealed in the historic Person of Christ. We must not ignore the claims of the Gospel records as the empirical Revelation of God in terms of human excellence, exemplified and taught. Far be it from us to hold lightly whatever of this has come into our hands.

But we must not forget the limitations of its scope, the change of social conditions, the veil of the kenosis, the questionings of criticism. The empirical does not as such enter into the realm of the absolute; and, interpreted by the Holy Spirit, only enters that realm together with the rest of the New Testament. God's self-revelation comes to us, certainly, through action, but the central act is the Act of Redemption. This Act is the focus of just that vision of God, life, duty, and the world that is the true orientation of man's life as God has made it; and we must make our particular adjustments to that vision as our judgement, thus enlightened, shall guide us. Within what limits we are able to draw from Christ's life and teaching a perennial supply of material for the reconstruction of human life, personal and social, can only be determined by experience; and those of us who are seeking to interpret the Gospel as the *absolute* truth cannot be asked to keep a gap open for it. Christ *has* revealed God. The supreme lessons of His life, and above all of the Cross, have been taught, and the answer of man's life has been "Video meliora proboque, deteriora sequor." Whatever may or may not be discovered for the enrichment of our ethics and the guidance of our lives, it remains true that all moral excellence, human and Divine, revolves somehow round the great ideals of Truthfulness, Purity, Justice, and Love, and that all these, in their different ways, are involved in the central Revelation of God. After all, He has created us in His own image, and, just so far as we see with the eyes of the New Creation, we see what He is and the world as He sees it.

The philosophical side of this is our task here; to get some understanding of how the primary idea of God as the supreme object of faith implies those particular ideas that we call His attributes, and how belief in Him is *ipso facto* belief in them.

I

We begin with *Personality*. Even orthodox writers are sometimes shy of attributing personality to God, because, to their minds, it seems unthinkable apart from limitation. And, of course, they have a right to ask what, in our view, is the exact significance of personality in God: for finite persons are known to us in their concrete individuality, under the circumstances of earthly life. What, in our knowledge of God, answers to human acquaintance? Spiritual communion with Him is transcendent and unique, and we cannot wonder that, in the eyes of some, it is rather degraded than otherwise by importing into it even the highest anthropomorphisms.

Most certainly we do not want to stand out for a word, without clear reason for assigning value to that word. But the word "person" does express a unique element in the idea of God, as we understand it, and the loss of it involves all sorts of minimizing substitutes. Power, life, spirit, and the like are all abstractions and further removed from the truly concrete idea than is personality, if we can but lay our hand upon its core of positive meaning.

Xenophanes, in a notable fragment, long ago objected to anthropomorphic Theism, on account of its arbitrary assimilation of the Deity to the human organism. Oxen, lions, and horses, he said, would depict God as like one of themselves. But, after all, would they not be right? That would be *for them* the true transition-point between the earthly and the Divine. And so to us is the human person. It is essential also, in our opinion, to say that God is superpersonal, for personality does not gather up *all* values. But, as it does not supersede all the beauty and meaning of the lower levels of creation, so neither is it superseded. Why, for instance, do we not say that God is a violet? Only because *we* cannot say it without belittling suggestions, not because, in its positive character, it is not true. We *can* say that God is personal, not only because this attribution is of great positive relevance, but because there is no higher form of reality known to us that it belittles. If we refuse to do so, the superpersonal easily becomes the sub-personal. We shall have more to say about superpersonality in a later chapter.

We can set forth what is really necessary to the completion of our argument without entering upon the whole great question of the meaning of personality in its various relations to surrounding ideas. The point we have reached is this: Personality is the highest form of concrete reality that we know, and, that being so, is inevitably taken up into our idea of God. And, further, this absorption does not imply that there is no type of being indefinitely higher, though it does deny that personal Theism is a mere symbolic or artificial makeshift of our thought. No, the fact that personality is that which, *for us*, stands highest in the scale of reality means that the absolute Highest meets us there, if at all. We cannot mount higher in our own house than the roof; and this, though it does not reach the sky, is open to it; for nothing opaque to *us* bars the view.

No soaring to higher categories can transcend the concreteness even of finite personality, which is anchored for ever to existential reality in the person of this, that, and the other living inhabitant of a world in which Philosophy itself is but an element and a growth. And, if so, it is clear that, when we contemplate infinite and absolute Being, known only in and through His own self-communication to us, the idea of personality needs not to be—and must not be—excluded or melted down. Our communication with God answers, on a higher plane, to our human intercourse, and *à fortiori* discloses to us *His* infinity and the infinite depth, in Him, of our own souls.

II

The attribution of *Goodness* to God does not (except in relation to the existence of Evil, of which we shall say something presently) offer any essential difficulty to those who believe in God, not first as the Absolute, but as the self-revealed Creator.

That our faith, in its fullest meaning, can only have as its object the supreme Being, and that the idea of this supreme Being, once accepted by faith, cannot be rationally brought within the sphere of the contingent or questionable we have already maintained. And surely it is hardly less obvious that this Being, unlike the "Absolute" that is above good and evil, must be absolutely good.

But, that we may not leave this entirely unargued, let us set it in the light of the faith-act itself. The supreme object of faith must be the supreme object of desire. And that which is for *me* the absolute object of desire—the desire behind and beyond all desires—is known to me *eo ipso* as the absolutely good, the Good-in-itself. The revelation that evokes the unique and crucial act—the totality-act—of faith is that of the ultimate Real and the ultimate Good in one.

It is well in this place to glance at the subject of Evil, and this may form also an introduction to our later treatment of the subject of Sin. And here we must make two assertions which may seem contradictory, but are in fact inseparable: evil is negation and evil is positive. Certainly it is not an illusion, for the illusion would be evil. It is essentially negating and destructive; but, just for that very reason, is not itself negative. True, it is the absence of good, but this absence means that goodness is not where it might have been, and that is a positive evil fact. Besides, how can definite sins—and pain also, considered in itself—be other than positively evil?

Evil, in the cause of destruction, becomes even constructive. Order in itself, as Augustine says with reference to the

Manichæans, is good. But Evil turns order against itself. A criminal gang is organized, and its organization may be good; it may embody much God-given skill: it may exploit even moral virtues, such as loyalty. Even this form of order, Augustine would rightly say, is, as order, good. But the particular order is, in its main character, evil. Thus Evil *embodies* itself. It is not an abstract principle swinging in mid-air. It is expressed in individual characters and in anti-social societies.

It has no *substantive* reality. But, dismissing Manichæan ideas, we still find ourselves Dualists. To deny the reality of Evil is to deny the reality of Good; for both members of an ultimate antithesis are ultimate.

Maintaining this dualism, the meaning of the idea of God comes home to us with far greater fullness and clarity, far greater consistency and reality, than without it. For now we understand it in antithesis to a principle that is not within God Himself, and is not the mere void encircling Him. No high conceptions of fatherly care and discipline, drawn from human character and life, can take the place of this. The idea of the righteous God is not simply a vast reflection in the clouds of the righteous man. If we may anticipate for a moment the subject of a later chapter, the ultimate meaning of Sin is revealed in the dualism of the Last Conflict and the Victory of the Resurrection. And, if of Sin, of all evil.

And this prepares us to meet a standing problem that has long dogged the footsteps of belief: we mean the very existence of evil, in view of the omnipotence of God. What seems remarkable, after all, is that the problem should have been so pressing, and for this reason: it arises from the apparent dilemma: God as deficient in love or as deficient in power; but the strange thing is that, not only by opponents, but even by troubled believers, the dilemma is for the most part promptly forgotten as such, and that in favour of the worse "horn" of it, as if there were no other. Yet it seems clear that Christian faith and experience rest far more upon

the Divine love and truth than upon omnipotence. Even
to accept the bare denial of the latter, apart from all further
definition, does not leave any such palpable and serious gap
in our belief as to threaten the main structure.

And, after all, for those who take the simple idea of
Creation as determinative of all our ideas about the relation
between God and man, mere abstract omnipotence is
irrelevant. Both the power of God and the correlative
possibility of external resistance are contained within the
implications of their creed. Mere blank omnipotence—
implying an *absolutely* plastic universe of real, conscious,
personal units—is unthinkable.

No great further burden is laid upon faith when we pass
from moral evil to pain. Even though we may be unable
satisfactorily to formulate a theory, true to logic and the
facts, of the connection between sin and suffering, yet, if
we have chosen to take our stand upon love, there is no
urgency about the definition of omnipotence. But here too
a word may be said which may link the problem of pain, if
not with what has been said already, at least with the sequel.

It has often been found helpful to turn to the thought of
the Divine Cross in face of all the evils that are rampant in
God's world. And the more or the less according to the view
that we take of it. It is not merely the idea of the Divine
suffering on which the solution depends, but just where and
how we lean our weight upon the *power* of God. Till we
understand the potence we cannot understand the omnipotence. We do not argue that God can do all things, and
therefore save us, but rather that God has saved us and therefore can do all things within the meaning of power. The Cross,
inwardly revealed at the centre of our world-view, is the
quintessence of the power of God. *There* is the key to all the
rest—suffering and sin. In that supreme experience of self-
verifying trust we know the power of the Saviour as that
of the Creator on another plane. Behind sovereign grace
is cosmic sovereignty. The Victory of the Resurrection,

with all its implications, shows to us the Divine power, not as abstract omnipotence, but conditioned, as all forms of power must be: shows it as expressed in an Act, an Act that is not just evidence, or symbol, or instance, of some reality outside itself, but is the direct primary object of our faith.

III

The idea of *Love* as expressed in the Greek Testament ἀγάπη emphasizes kindness and benevolence, without giving prominence to individual and personal love and the desire for communion. Yet we need hardly hesitate to take it in its widest and deepest sense, which is certainly that involved in the Christian idea of God. In any case, it is not a mere matter of the will, as sometimes said. Its acts spring from feeling and mental disposition. They are its credentials, not itself. It is in emotion that its essence is glimpsed.

If for the moment we present the matter in the light of the more abstract thinking, we would say of Love that it is the full expression, in the sphere of emotion and concrete relationship, of Unity in Otherness. The more it penetrates to the innermost essence of the other—beneath even the most fundamental *qualities*—the more is it truly love. No perfect phenomenon of it exists on earth. But to find it— so far as we can find it—we must first take the nature of its *object* into account. We speak of love in all sorts of connection: of the love of art, of truth, of flowers, of eating. This is not because the thin common element is the essential meaning of the word (love in itself is infinitely deep and full), but because the full meaning shades off toward nothing as our thought moves from the larger and higher objects to the narrower or more abstract. A game, or profession, for instance, is only loved—except sentimentally—in the sense that we take pleasure in engaging in it.

But, though human love does but imperfectly express all that love is, we can see guiding lines and the direction in which they converge. The idea, for instance, of two souls united by love into one appeals to the simplest mind. We may even take this as our starting-point, and simply try to show how its formulation is often imperfect. It is imperfect in so far as the unity is regarded as in some way superseding or modifying the duality. That implies either that the phrase is considered a metaphor or that a common-sense qualification must be understood. In other words, it either must not be taken too literally or not pressed too far. In any case, the unity is emphasized, the duality taken for granted, not reflected on. And, of course, a reflective mind also, if inclined to a mystical Monism, may disparage otherness, not thus naïvely, but explicitly, and see in love something like a universal fusion. "Lo, there is neither mortal nor immortal: nought is on earth or in the heavens but love." If, however, we adhere closely to the precise idea of Creation, as it shines in the light of re-creative Redemption, the philosophy of Love stands out in greater clarity and coherence, while still the naïve insight remains, on its positive side, true. The creature is an entity, even relatively to the Creator, and therefore certainly to other creatures. Love is unity in otherness, with the emphasis no less on the otherness than on the unity. It is not otherness minimized by unity. For individuality, as it is not selfishness on the one hand, is not a mere warehouse of "contributions" on the other: it is the being an individual—a unit of Reality, correlated with other units.

But this, so far, is only the static side of the matter. Creation is dynamic. And love, so far as its desires are not yet realized, is dynamic. The two aims of love are unity and benefaction. It is in respect of the former that we best see the difference in kind between Divine and human love, which is this: man's love seeks unity between two given others: God's love makes otherness out of a given unity. It is God's love that is, in the absolute sense, creation. All the perfections in human nature—man's life itself—God has in

Himself: it is the new entity, the new individual, the new other, that He creates.

IV

We now come to the attribute of *Holiness*, which it is vital not to evade. It is tempting here to criticize the critics of Otto's celebrated treatise on the subject, which we believe to stand unmoved by them. But this is not essential to our present purpose; and, since the attribution of holiness to God is generally accepted in the abstract, it may suffice to bring out the positive idea by way of a brief examination of certain imperfect modes of understanding it.

(1) It has been said that "holiness" is a term indicating our feeling toward God, and not anything in God Himself. It is not said to be untrue, but to be subjective. But where —as here—the reference is to an external Object, the purely subjective is the untrue. Even if we endeavour to express it in terms of our worship and adoration, we are obliged to say that God is such that He produces these feelings in us. And that is to predicate something of His character. For surely the bare fact of our re-acting thus to Him is utterly non-significant, if the experience of worship and of reverence does not answer within itself to what He is. The numinous is certainly *in* the mind; but, as we have seen earlier, if it is not also somewhere outside, it is a spiritual hallucination.

(2) It is said that Love and Holiness are the same. What is meant by this assertion? The content of the two ideas is certainly not identical: when we say the one we do not mean the other. Is it meant that they are different aspects of the same thing? But of what third thing are they the aspects? The fact surely is that those who say this are virtually denying holiness in order to do fuller justice, as they think, to love, to capture for it some of the emotional reaction that holiness evokes.

(3) Holiness is admitted as the attribute of an attribute. God's love, it is said, is a holy love. But this again, taken by

itself, is an unconscious evasion. It is quite true that God's love is a holy love; but that is because love and holiness are united in the unity of the Divine nature, not because one of them is predicable of God through the other, or because God's love is a species within a genus. Either *God* is, Himself, in the direct sense, holy, or He is not.

(4) Holiness is explained by human holiness, seen in God by His requirement of it in us. Again, we have nothing to say against this, except as a disposal of the question before us. In the previous case, holiness is discovered as an attribute of another Divine attribute, here as an ideal of human character. But holiness in man is not just like other virtues. God is the Holy ("das Heilige"). Other virtues have a relative independence. It is true that love, for instance (in accordance with what we have said about the Divine *à priori*), could never have been known to us even in man—and indeed even man could never have been known to us—had not these ideas been created in us by the Archetype of them all. But in the case of holiness more than this has to be said. The idea of God is not merely latent in it, but explicit. An Atheist believes in love, but he cannot really believe in holiness. Holiness in man has direct reference to the transcendent God, and is first a relation to Him. That the word also describes a quality of human character cannot of course be denied. But in man it is a religious quality. Godward, it lives by worship: manward, it lives by glorifying God. But God is not religious: He is the Object of religion. Therefore the human quality is not, as a quality, the key to the understanding of the Divine.

Holiness is just the Godhead of God, presupposed by all the other qualities predicated of Him—God as designated rather than described. Even a finite person is not a bundle of adjectives. True, "holy" is itself an adjective: we say "God is holy". But this is tautology; a much needed tautology, for it is not superfluous to say "God is God". To much religious sentiment of to-day God is everything but Divine.

CHAPTER IX

SIN

I

Sin is committed against *God*. Sin *as such* is not committed against finite persons, or against laws, even the laws of God simply as laws—though it is the breach of them, or against the purposes of God—though it obstructs them, but against God Himself. To say that it is committed against God "personally" has far greater truth, but even this is really redundant and by itself may tend to anthropomorphism. But still less must we be satisfied with lower categories, as if God might be sinned against, but impersonally; for instance, as Lawgiver. What we have said does not imply that all sin is definite rebellion against God, but that sin is wrongdoing *in its character as* committed against God.

It is true to say that sin is of the nature of ingratitude or unlovingness toward the Author of all our good. But it is not adequate. We cannot explain sin by reducing it to moral ugliness. Thus, it cannot be *defined* as selfishness, whether toward God or toward Man, for selfishness, first, is sin. But let us look a little closer.

Two convergent ideas, which, though convergent, never unite except in the highest Theism, may help us to formulate the completed idea of Sin; that of *wrong* (as when we use the verb "to wrong") and that of *violation*. When we say that sin is committed (in general at any rate) against persons and also that it is committed against a principle, or law, of Goodness, or Righteousness, we are using the word "against" in these two different senses respectively. But each meaning has a sub-reference to the other. When an individual is wronged, *he* is wronged, but his rights are *violated*. The act committed has the double characteristic of being purposely detrimental and of being illicit. But these two characteristics are not separate, even as reason and consequent are separate: the act is the proper subject not simply of censure but of *protest*: that is to say the violated law of Righteousness is as it were embodied *pro tanto* in the wronged person. But, on the other hand, it is the law itself, which is above both parties, that is violated. That it should be possible to wrong a man, who himself is no source or representative of this eternal law, exhibits this transcendence of the imperative of Righteousness even as against social obligation, and even though we regard social obligation as necessarily implied in all duty.

But this conception of the violated moral law is itself cut short. We have seen in the chapter on Ethics that the conception of Goodness as the duty behind all duties is the culminating point of Ethics, and that nevertheless its abstractness, if it is not met from another direction, condemns it in the end to unreality. For Goodness could not personalize itself in the claims of finite individuals if it had not its own claim. This implies personality, and Righteousness is not personal except as an aspect of a larger Reality in which even the transcendence of the moral law is gathered up. Such personality—the personality of the Superpersonal—must be absolute, ultimate, and supreme, resting no claims on anything deeper or higher than itself. Wrongdoing assumes in relation to God an eternal and transcendent character, answering to the Divine holiness with which it is confronted.

We cannot here attempt to demonstrate the impregnability on all sides of our conclusions, as if we were writing primarily on Ethics or Apologetics. We have attempted only to give an indication of how, for those who have followed us sympathetically so far, the more partial and abstract conceptions, in Ethics as elsewhere, may be seen as integrated in the central view-point of Christian Theism.

II

This chapter will be mainly devoted to the relation between the personal and racial elements of sin. This is a most important, and also very difficult subject: and, before we can bring these two aspects together, it is essential to exhibit the irreducible distinction between them.

The sinfulness of the race appears in the individual in the form of sub-conscious perversities, of corrupted desires, of every sort of tendency to do things that are wrong in themselves. These, though they lead to actual sins, may even deprive them of their actuality, by perverting the moral judgement. A religious persecutor, for instance, who commits an unquestionably evil act with the full conviction that he is doing the will of God, and that he would be sinning if he did not so act, is under the influence of an immorality—whether regarded as his own or as traditional—which has captured his conscience itself. We hardly realize what a paradox this presents. The man is sinning because he is committing a sin, and yet he would be sinning if he did not commit it, for he would be going against his conscience. It does not avail to say—though this is true—that his conscience is defiled and darkened. For we have no better guide at any given moment than our conscience, however fallible, and its authorities as it accepts and understands them. The fact is that we cannot, by any possibility, fuse these two affirmations. We *can* only say that in one respect the man sins in performing the act and in another he sins in not performing it. But this is not a mere confession of our failure to think the question out. It shows us that there are two sides to sin which are not reducible one to the other, and that any theory that ignores either, or tries to fuse them, is wrong. Our aim, therefore, must be so to understand the idea of sin that the two counter-propositions appear as the complementary sides of one indivisible Divine truth. If sin is, in its full meaning, divinely revealed *ipso facto* in the revelation of the Gospel, then the idea of it cannot be expected to disclose all its sides simultaneously upon the lower dimensional level of human reflection.

Now let us observe how entirely meaningless and unreal each of these aspects of sin is without the other. Even racial sin—if it is sin at all—must have in it some implication of rebellion, or lawlessness. Distorted tastes, impulses, and desires, hatred, impurity, and meanness, as conditions of the mind, would not be regarded as sinful but for their tendency to action, be it only mental action. The crisis of conscious temptation may not have yet come; but the will is weakened for the conflict already. This is a commonplace in itself, but it means more than that evil states and evil deeds are interwoven. Evil states and dispositions *are* implicit evil acts. Freewill, only expressed in face of a sharp issue, is, under time conditions, partly latent. And, when we add to this that to succumb to temptation is to enhance the evil state, we are contemplating an interaction of two factors so close that, the more we consider it, the more it appears that we are handling abstractions from a more concrete truth that lies further back. An act has no real and ultimate moral significance if it does not spring at all from the character of the agent, nor yet again if it is *wholly* predetermined therein; which it would be if it could not make some change in it (that is, in him), whether for good or for evil. All this applies to sin as we know it in this world of relativity and Time, where it is already there.

We have not yet used the term "Original Sin", for we have been working up to it. Sinfulness, as an empirical fact, is obvious to all to whom sin means anything. It is commonly thought sufficient to explain it by reference, on the one hand, to inherited tendencies that have outlived their evolutionary functions, and, on the other, to the effects of personal sin. But this is too superficial. At the most it can only explain how what we call sins came about. But to call them sins presupposes the reality of *Sin* as such. It is its meaning,

rather than its empirical origin, that we first need to understand. The doctrine of the Fall is not an explanation in that
sense, though it points to what we have to think of as past.
It follows rather than precedes that of Original Sin. But it is
in the end a necessity of thought, and it is coming into its own
again. It cannot be reduced to a thin theory of atavistic
survivals. But neither does it depend on any speculative
venture. Theories, however, of pre-natal sin, corporate or
individual, are not necessarily mere speculation. Considered
as attempts to extract, and exhibit in its purity, the essence of
a faith entangled in really irrelevant difficulties, they have
a claim to close attention. And modern theology might
move faster in the end if it stopped to analyse these theories,
instead of lightly dismissing them.

Actual sins and sins unknown as such to the person committing them, must certainly be distinguished. But even
actual sins may be committed with many degrees of consciousness. Sins do not lend themselves to rigid classification
as tangible facts. The two types stand for two *aspects* of Sin,
which, as we are trying to show, must be seen in sharp
distinction and in complete mutual dependence. And, if so,
the Fall is a mysterious presupposition, which, however, is
reflected in the characteristics of both: in the universality,
continuity, and depth of original sin and in the wilfulness
and guilt of actual sin. All explanations of the genesis of Sin
which do more than indicate the convergence of lines of
thought towards what is *necessarily* a mystery can be proved
untenable.

If, for instance, the relics of the "ape and tiger" congenital
in us merely *set the task* for conscious morality: merely
confronted us from outside as an enemy to be resisted: the
Fall would still have to be postulated, but with a difference,
and in the teeth of reality. It would be a definite transition
in the life of every sinner, a biographical tragedy. Temptation
would be explicit and sudden: there would be no degrees of
responsibility. Conscience, undefiled and unblinded, would

see the issue clearly and at once. But this is not so. The Ego
and the sources of temptation are not in clear antithesis.
There is that within the Ego that opens the backdoor. Sin
itself is congenital, therefore racial.

On the other hand, as the Archbishop of York has
pointed out, the Fall cannot be understood simply in terms
of the rebellious will. His own theory, however, is not
adequate. Sin has arisen from the original self-centredness
of personality. "This whole personality in action is the will;
and it is the will which is perverted.... It is the form taken
by our knowledge of good and evil that perverts our nature.
We know good and evil, but we know them amiss. We
take them into our lives, but we mis-take them. The corrup-
tion is at the centre of rational and purposive life."[1] But errors
about moral good and evil—considered apart from mere
errors about facts that happen to be relevant to our particular
moral judgements—would surely be impossible to any
hitherto sinless being. This is to presuppose what needs to
be explained.

Feeling, will, and knowledge all seem candidates for the
prior place in the explanation of Sin. We cannot see the
solution otherwise than as a religious doctrine. It is behind
all psychology. The mind is baffled in the application of its
self-discovered laws when these pass into the larger whole
of personality, seen (where alone it can be fully seen) in
relation to its Creator. We must keep in view all along the
super-historic and super-scientific level upon which Theology
must plant its feet. The doctrine of Sin no more belongs
to the departmental mind than it refers to the departmental
man. To explain it from empirical standpoints is not
free thinking, but bondage to the historic or scientific
imagination.

The doctrine is also super-philosophical; but Philosophy
can at least learn its own place in the hierarchy of knowledge.
To take philosophic truth as the highest and most concrete

[1] *Nature, Man and God*, p. 367.

truth is a philosophic error: therefore that it is *not* is a *philosophic* truth. To it alone in man, the Gospel, once accepted by faith, is, in the fullest sense, the *wisdom* of God: and, if the Gospel, then its revelation of the meaning of Sin.

That meaning is a unit of experience. Its two aspects are realized in worship, repentance, and forgiveness. To repent purely of actual sin is not only entirely shallow and inadequate, but makes repentance limited, variable, and qualified (not to say more at present); for all repentance implies that the act repented of comes "from the heart". Sins are not a matter for repentance apart from sinfulness. But neither is sinfulness apart from sins. It has been said that, in the course of spiritual growth, we come to repent rather of what we are than of what we do. One can see the truth in this; but repentance is not solely a change of mind and attitude, even when we couple with this an abhorrence of the state abandoned. It is essentially self-condemnation, or self-blame. It is the confession of *guilt*, and we cannot be guilty of a state, except as brought about by oneself.

Sin is essentially personal on the side of the sinner. "*I* have sinned"; and whatever *I* do in relation to God—whatever *I* am responsible to Him for—is in some way the act or thought of my indivisible self. At some point, in some way, this or that particular sin, if it is sin at all, is *mine* absolutely, even though I myself may be conscious only of a vague culpability, an unlocated stain, hidden by very tolerable excuses. And indeed we often sin in such a way that utter self-condemnation would be really unmeaning; yet the absoluteness of sin as sin remains. What this means is that all actual sins are more or less abstract features of what the old theology rightly called the "fallen state". Original sin, even where it automatically expresses itself in action, cannot be personal as between man and God, and therefore is not by itself truly sin. But by virtue of it sins *are* sins.

And this central sinfulness, or perverted nature, in each of us is truly racial; not merely, in the ordinary acceptance of the term, individual, even though pre-natal. For the individual *is* racial, and that which lies deepest in the heart of our individual being is also universal. Monists are not wrong in making the Whole as deep as the individual, they are only wrong in making it deeper.

Here we find the true solidarity of mankind in its sin: not in the fiction of vicarious repentance or corporate guilt, or the organized "national humiliation" that was demanded during the War. The unrepentant cannot be represented in the repentance of another.

That original sin would be meaningless without actual sin may seem less necessary to urge than the converse; since the very idea of original sin has all it can do to commend its own claim, and—one might think—could never usurp the entire field. That is true, but just because this idea has to struggle for recognition, it is more than ever important to understand what it really means, and to repudiate all claims that it does not really make. For, although few would accept it as the whole truth, yet it might seem to stand, as it were, side by side with that of actual sin, and complicate the situation. Whereas they lean upon one another.

In all the deepest repentance the two elements are visibly present. There are no irreducible units of experience that exhibit one or the other by itself. But, further, as in all such cases, when once the experience is reflectively grasped, one can go on to understand how it *must* be so. Original sin in itself—even though we think of it as strictly our own—tends rather to modify than to stimulate repentance. It gives an excuse—yes, and a valid excuse. Actual sin, which is the result, *yet not irresistible result*, of it, is involved.

And is not actual sin even *presupposed* in our sinful state? If so, are we not led into some theory of pre-natal guilt?[1] Is there, after all, essential truth in the idea mystically ex-

---

[1] It has in fact been argued (apart from theology) that the blame-worthiness of any action implies that it has partly been caused by previous action, and so points back to pre-natal existence.

pressed by saying that we all severally "sinned in Adam"? If so, we need not shrink back from this consequence, so long as we let it hang loose as a corollary, and firmly refuse it as a speculation upon which the theological doctrine may be based. At any rate, this actual sin runs into the present and repeats itself in our particular transgressions. If it did not, we should feel ourselves released from any responsibility even for our own pre-natal fall.

In short, original and actual sin are distinguishable but inseparable moments in one simple meaning, as it is directly known in religious experience, and in that alone. The unification cannot be too close, so long as we approach it from both sides.

III

And this brings us to our next point. That the meaning of sin is coherent only behind the distinction of original and actual is reflected in the temporal conditions of Repentance. We could never repent of the past simply as past. All sense of guilt surely implies, not simply a sort of mystic qualitative defilement, but imperfect change of will. Repentance is bound to be imperfect. That is why it is possible at all. Perfect repentance would perish in the vacuum of its own creating. It would pass directly, not into a devout consciousness of Divine forgiveness, but into self-complacency. The sin repented of still clings. Our several sins are not absolutely self-contained units. In respect of particular sins, it is true, the release may really be accomplished. Repentance may complete its work. But, so long as the repentance is there— and in some form it must always be there—it must be imperfect or it cannot be at all. If it were complete, it would not be only a passing flash—that would not matter if it did its work—but literally durationless: that is, it could not occur in Time at all. But it does occur in Time, and often is, and needs to be, protracted. Sin first, then repentance, is the logical order; but we never see either in its essence apart from the other. Sin is most revealed when in the death-clutch of repentance: repentance is always marred by sin.

But there is another side to this. If repentance is not complete, it has already begun, and so God's work has begun. Repentance comes by the grace of God. This, as we shall see, is vital to the idea of the Atonement. But it brings us face to face with a difficulty. While, on the one hand, the deepest sense of sinfulness—often, no doubt, in perverted and morbid forms—is, in its efficacy, a matter not only of doctrine but of experience, we sometimes, on the other hand, seem, by our very repentance, to be raised above the need of repentance, so that the very fact and sincerity of our confession weakens its own force and qualifies its own reality.

But such difficulties belong to the sphere of reflection, and the experiences upon which we reflect are suspended—or at least projected—for the purpose of reflection. It is only within the experience itself—as with all spiritual experiences —not when outside it or half outside it, that we can expect to touch reality. In respect of transgressions severally, repentance really does tend to move out of itself. But its own imperfection needs repentance, and so *ad infinitum*. Even when it does, after a time, sever us from some particular sin, and make it to be a thing of the dead past, we know that that sin was only a unit of our pervading sinfulness. We may indeed progress spiritually and morally, but this progress is progress in the depth and reality of our repentance. Once allowed to feed upon itself, to draw its inspiration and strength lower down the stream than the eternal fountain-head of forgiving and redeeming Love, where we mingle with publicans and sinners, then, however impressive, it loses its distinctive Christian mark. We never leave behind us the call to say: "We are not worthy so much as to gather up the crumbs under Thy Table."

Repentance and all forms of spiritual revolt against sin are incipient spiritual victory, and for this very reason tend to veil rather than reveal our sin, *as* ours, when once the experience contained within it fades. Yet, at the heart of the experience, we have no such delusion. There act and state are one. Actual sins are never purely actual, and a sinful condition is not sinful purely in its passive and adjectival character. If the state were only a state, it would merely excuse the act: if the act were only an act, it would be dead before it could be repented of. But, if they are one, and if, as we have seen, the state is racial and super-individual, so also, in some mysterious manner, is the act. We are thus brought to the doctrine of the Fall—*to* it simply, for we shall never penetrate into it, or walk round it.

IV

This radical doctrine of Sin has a position of special advantage in relation to the others, just *because* it insists upon the central and therefore pervasive hold of sin upon the human heart. Most certainly it does not maintain the delusiveness of natural human goodness. If it did, it would make sin to appear not more real but less, for disease cannot feed upon a corpse. But it declares, and *consistently* maintains, that man as man, and therefore the highest in man, is fallen. And, if this be so, all protests on the part of the most spiritual minds, and on behalf of the loftiest ideals, against its emphasis upon sin find, upon its own principles, a full explanation. Sin exploits the best, and if we find mystics of the highest type, apostles of love, holy and devoted Christians, sometimes demurring to the severe hamartiology of St Paul, we need not be surprised. And, when it is said that such teaching obscures pure ethics by the motive of fear, disparages the love of God, or creates a one-sided and straitened religious life, we must remember that both its assailants and its adherents are thinking all the time under the conditions of the Fall; and that, moreover, the adherents have this advantage: they keep more steadily in view the human blindness and infirmity that hamper us as we try to follow up the meaning of God's truth; for that is part of their doctrine itself, and not a shadow cast on it from another context of thought. Opinion is transcended in the total suspension of intellectual claims till we have listened to the voice of God. Till then, reason has not found its datum. Till then, the radical doctrine cannot be met without begging the question. Sin, it is true, is not apprehended in a direct act of faith, as if it were an object of trust and self-committal. But it is the underside, or negative side, of that object. It is apprehended as that from which, primarily, we are saved.

Liberal Theism is not an answer to that doctrine, for the latter begins where Liberalism leaves off. Those who hold the radical view may argue that the relatively minimizing theories are the outcome of arrested thinking. Once admit that the idea of Sin belongs to the theological, or religious, plane of thought, and not to the merely ethical, and this determines our entire conception: Sin is viewed *sub specie æternitatis*: it is understood in terms of the alienation of man, at the centre of his being, from God.

V

The idea of Sin will receive further treatment in the course of our study of its relation to other central Christian ideas in the ensuing chapters. But one thing may be said here which should link this chapter with the next. We may start with the idea of Redemption. (This is, according to our method, a perfectly valid procedure. It means only that the two ideas, Sin and Redemption, are interlocked in the unity of the one organic truth *revealed* first in its wholeness.) In other words, corporate Redemption presupposes corporate sin, in the radical sense here maintained. Differing types of Christianity agree in this: that the salvation of man is not simply a process initiated, but a gift won and a victory achieved, by the Cross and the Resurrection. It is plausible, no doubt, to hold simply that, since the sinful state of man was a fact when Christ came into the world, a Divine Event might have been enacted within rather than upon the race—an act which should transform its prospects, initiate a process of renewal within it, and provide for the regeneration of its individuals down the ages. In that case there would be no need to postulate a fallen condition in the race itself, such as would call for a direct and single act of racial Redemption. The avoidance of a mystic realism in our conception of the race might seem at first sight to commend this idea rather than the other.

It is well to have referred to this view at the present early stage, though the answer to it will develop as we go on, and though, in any case, it is directed only against our last proposition. Here we will just indicate our position. It is, that the redemptive acts—which are one act—*are* to be regarded as directly performed upon humanity by God in the Person of Jesus Christ, and not merely as the initiation of a process and the inauguration of a new economy. Otherwise He could not be the present Saviour of the individual in the full sense that the solifidian doctrine demands. The faith of the individual finds in Him the clue even to itself: yields to taking that began even before itself began—before life began—deep in the depths where "all is each and each is all". We hope that, when we come to treat of the Incarnation, it will be seen that no fiction of an abstract race-entity is here assumed. That would be quite contrary to our method and views. But it is from the soteriological side that the completion of the thoughts of this chapter must come.

CHAPTER X

SALVATION (I)

The old naïve teaching about Salvation very naturally (and very rightly) assumed that to be saved is to be saved *from*: it was primarily deliverance from eternal death. Modern teaching (also quite rightly) would have us remember that we are saved *unto*—God, righteousness, service. The old teaching did not for a moment forget the positive side, but sometimes tended to regard it as rather consequence of, or sequel to, salvation than a part of it. But is it not rather true that the Divine absolution and the Divine renewal are but abstractions from the one concrete Act of God in Christ?

There is one note of emphasis that we have been losing, and, in losing it, we have allowed the very conception of right and wrong to drop to a lower level. The old teaching was not satisfied to depict the consequences of sin as terrible to the good man, or to the man to whom sin was already the enemy: they were terrible to the bad man. It said bluntly, with St Paul, that the wages of sin is death.

Now we are quite sure that salvation cannot be understood without clear reference to its background, or negative side: or, in other words, to its primary appeal to man, not as good, or latently good, or wishing to be good, but on the *ultimate* ground of his need and his sin. It matters not how little we know about this background. We may advance or draw in the boundary-line of our thought, but it is always there, and is itself the contact of the Beyond. The acceptance of our nescience, here as elsewhere, is but the definition of the content of our knowledge.

But then over against this we must set the secondary, but quite essential, aspect of salvation, its relation to the time-process of moral and spiritual renewal. Each implies the other. We begin with the former, that is to say, with the problem of man in his totality, of sin as such, of the ultimate issue: or, in older language, with the direct relation of pardon to the "Last Judgement".

I

There is one thing that must here be said, and said very decidedly. As soon as we come to salvation in its absolute character—as distinguished from the removal of moral and spiritual inhibitions—we are faced with a peculiar modern perversity, towards which—with all desire to be sympathetic to those who differ from us—we cannot pretend to feel tolerant. Reproofs or gibes levelled at those who are concerned with their own salvation are a mockery of the human soul and of the Divine Gospel. And yet they are sometimes given forth as if they were homiletical truth above controversy. Why, in religion only, is self-regard, simply as such, treated as identical with selfishness? And what Gospel have we for others if we have none for ourselves?

It is certain the self-regarding motive cannot be eliminated from the ideals of religion, any more than from the New Testament. Supported by misuse and imperfect understanding of the refutation of false psychological Hedonism, some of us have adopted with strange favour that monstrosity of abstraction, the ideal of the purely altruistic man, and launched a gospel that is all transport and no goods. The quest that we are called to stimulate and assist is held up to scorn and censure.

Whatever perverted high-mindedness there is in this, one of its ingredients, surely, is unbelief. We are not called upon to produce high motives for seeking God, only to believe that He will give them to us when we have found Him.[1] An act of kindness is none the less pure in motive, none the less charged with the sentiments and impulses of love, because it would never have been performed had not the

---

[1] See paragraph on Goodness-as-such, Ch. VI, section II.

soul tasted of the joy of its own deliverance and of its own
sure and certain hope.

And not only at the beginning, or at the earlier stages, is
this self-regarding motive implicitly co-present with all other
motive that is there. An ultimate aim is not a mere bull's-eye:
it is *sought*; and whatever we seek we seek *for self*, even though
it be the good or gratification of others. The will to have, or
enjoy, is implied in the idea of purpose. And the supreme
object of search is God, who can never be a mere means to
an end, even to a moral end. True, He cannot be a mere
means to our own happiness: this would be the real fallacy
of psychological Hedonism: but our happiness is *in* Him—in
Him by the very essence of His being and ours. The mere
search for happiness in itself is a perversion and abstraction
of our sin-warped minds, just because happiness *is* not in
itself, but in God. And *there* it is the other side of the
converted will.

The question "What if my own salvation—or my own
good—and that of others *were* in final opposition? Would
I be obliged to regard the unselfish course as irrational?"
is no doubt at the background of much of this, and we shall
do well to face it out. But the true way to face it out is to
challenge it directly as a pseudo-question; because it supposes
a situation which, from the standpoint of a rightly grounded
Christian belief, is radically impossible. A supposed situation
in which Ethics is true but the Gospel untrue—or even
metaphysical truth not true—is pseudo-situation. The solution of the last crux of Ethics, as with Philosophy, comes
from outside it. Within it, self-reference and self-denial
demand an ultimate synthesis, but can never rise above their
relative conflict. The solution of the ego-centric problem in
Ethics—where it is as real as in Epistemology—lies in this:
that God *has*, by His own action, given to men the gift of
that which He seeks from them: and that gift transcends the
opposition of self-reference and self-denial, transmuting the
antithesis into concentric union. We need the spiritual and

intellectual courage to accept the Gospel as the *ne plus ultra* of first principles, none the less though it is factual and paradoxical. That is part of its paradox.

The Gospel as the emancipation of man to be what God created him to be—the finite image of Himself, points to the ultimate and ideal fulfilment of the man's own desires. We therefore make no apology for treating it as such and not as a special form of emotional morality. We are sure that our modern "gospel of adventure", our "romance of selfless-ness"—all our temperamental thrills—will not do the work of a thankful acceptance of the Unspeakable Gift. It is the cry of a decadent faith.

Nor need we be repelled by the apparently negative import of the word "salvation". It is not so much that this can be *supplemented* by due emphasis upon the gifts that are ours in Christ, here and hereafter. Since our quest is above all things for integral unity of thought, let us rather ask whether the very idea of salvation, or deliverance, is not, in its very negativity, positive. We shall see this easily if we steadily keep in view the meaning of *Creation*, with all the infinity of its purpose, which salvation restores and guarantees. That which is the negation of negation is positive. But we have already, in dealing with faith, brought this point forward, so that there is no need to say more about it here. We must, however, emphasize the *restoration* of the creative act. To treat Redemption as *continuous* with that act—whatever dis-tinctions we may draw within the continuity—is a betrayal to mere Natural Religion. God's approach, in Christ, to the natural order as a whole—therefore from outside it—and including the very ideas about it in our minds, is the very position that we are seeking throughout to make good. And the more consistently we view the *whole* content of the natural order, physical and spiritual—including all the *élan vital* that it has within itself—as the subject of an external saving Act, the more completely does the positive import of that Act, even defined in terms of deliverance, appear.

God restores the efficacy of His purpose in nature by rescuing the units of that purpose from eternal death. That is the plain blunt truth, and there is no possibility of watering it down. If we reduce the Fall to deflection and dislocation, we reduce correspondingly our idea of salvation, and a reduced soteriology is no dam against a flood of immanentalist thought that in the end would sweep away all that is distinctive in Christianity. But if Redemption is taken seriously as the restoration of the *creature* as such, both ideas are preserved intact.

It is just because of the eternal depth in each man's being, the intensive infinity of even the finite soul, as God's creature, that eternal death has a transcendent and pregnant import, not only moral and psychological. To *start* from this idea of death as a subjective condition is to start—in meaning though not in time—too low down the stream. As such it does not exclude the possibility of a euthanasia, or even perhaps of a very comfortable non-moral paradise continuing for ever. It is just the fact—the provisional, anomalous, unstable fact—of the co-existence of death toward God with life upon God's earth that shakes conscience to its foundations. The present state of spiritual death has a meaning in it correlated with the deepest meaning of the human soul: we must view the former as well as the latter *sub specie æternitatis*. That which begins further back than evolution fulfils itself beyond it.

The ultimate goal of sin differs radically from disciplinary punishment. It is, as we often and truly say, the inevitable end of persistence in living apart from God. But this is not the whole that is to be said. We must not level down religious truth to mere biological law. The tragedy of the situation is that human vitality, self-consciousness, development—even the life of the spirit in the wider sense—does not just wilt away in the absence of the Divine presence at the centre. It may thrive under the curse. The Kingdom of God does not come to its own simply through the peaceful decay of all that will not be assimilated to it. The tares not only wait but grow until the harvest. Great and high things must be shaken that the things that are not shaken may remain.

II

When we think of death, we always, fundamentally, mean annihilation. When we regard it otherwise, we are, so far, not thinking of it as death at all. And the higher the life, the deeper the descent of death. Dr Johnson was essentially right when he said that all men fear death, but some put it away from their minds more than others. Now Christianity is the awakener of self-consciousness. It makes the soul to stand out in its own unfathomable reality. And death in its real inwardness appears when that appears which is its ultimate antithesis; namely, the true life, the life not only of the old creation—self-conscious humanity—but of the new. Death is not negative, but negation—supremely positive because it is the supreme negation.

It may help to make clear our position if we glance at a subject which otherwise would hardly lie within our scope, the general question of human immortality. We venture to hold views upon the nature of the question which do not agree with the usual assumptions both of those who attack or doubt and of those who defend the affirmative answer. The subject may be approached from various sides; and we have previously published our conclusions on one and another of them. Here it is the essential character of the issue at stake that concerns us. Confining ourselves to this, it may not be impossible to indicate briefly the position to which converging lines of thinking have brought us.

To start with, we may say of Philosophy in this connection what we have said of it already in relation to Religion. That is, that it never keeps true even to itself if it forgets that it is a *department* of man—even of the individual man; and therefore the true Ego, the *punctum individuationis*, continually transcends it. The very appearance of this within Philosophy, necessary as it is, compromises its self-evidence.

And empirical Science too is essentially disqualified for any fundamentally negative pronouncement on this matter. The soul is not—just as God is not—a contingent entity at all. By its meaning it is not this, whether we believe in it or not. Science cannot handle the real Ego. All that is said in its name amounts only to this: that there is no reason to believe that the soul is immortal. And even this it is not entitled to say.

For let it be noted, in the first place, that we cannot affirm the abstract non-existence of anything. Our rejections of the wildest absurdities are refusals *in limine* to admit the question. The negative answer to a live question is fundamentally different from the rejection of one that is still-born, however difficult it may be to draw the line between the particular examples of each. We disbelieve in innumerable things simply because they have no place in the general scheme of thought and being as we understand it. These disbeliefs are practically absolute, because the question of existence outside that scheme would be a dead question, excluded *in limine*. We should not accept any arbitrary assertion of the existence of something somewhere in the universe, merely because, being so far removed from our world, we could not adduce any positive arguments against even its probability. But belief in the real soul, or Ego, has its own inherent truth-claim. Merely to reject it as a dead issue has no meaning for those to whom it is a very living issue. To undermine this or that particular ground of confidence which Science or ordinary experience seems to provide is no positive disproof of the existence of that which, by hypothesis, is uniquely related to all experience.

Even the vaguest inklings and intimations of immortality have thus a peculiar advantage of their own. If indeed they are themselves used as arguments, psychopathical explanations may rob them of their force. But the attack cannot be carried into their stronghold, where the actual intuiting takes place. The right course in all such cases is—not to hug our intuitions in the dark, but to hold them up in the face of all relevant criticism and attack, retreating with them, if we have to retreat, ever farther back into the inarticulate, till, concentrated and purified, they disclose their true relation to the world of thought and experience from which the first challenge to them came.

But to return to our main track. We are still considering the general subject of immortality. Passing into a less rarefied atmosphere, we may now briefly note two very familiar difficulties, and see how they stand in relation to what has already been said. So far we have regarded the soul as a transcendent entity, which as such holds its own ultimate credentials in its own hands, and cannot even be questioned on ordinary empirical grounds without prejudicing the issue. We have now to take into account the fact that this transcendent entity does express itself in psychic occurrences and through a material organ.

First the psychic side, the assumption that absolute death, that is, annihilation—whether in fact it takes place or not—can be conceived by simply supposing the cessation of the psychic stream. So conceived, it would be empirically possible. For the cessation of consciousness seems at least a tenable idea, and might even be maintained, on empirical grounds, to be probable. And, since an unconscious and insensible soul is unthinkable, such cessation would carry with it the annihilation of the soul.

Now on one point we agree. We hold that the survival of death does involve the retention, or resumption, of our present stream of consciousness. We do not believe in a soul-entity that forgets all and begins afresh. But we still maintain that the reality of the soul over against the sphere of its earthly life and death is rightly immune from empirical doubt. The difficulty seems to lie partly in the reference to the future. Can a future event be immune, on principle, from such doubt? Is not our survival—not to say our immortality

—a contingency, and therefore perhaps an improbability? So it would be if the simple flow of consciousness were all that the soul is, or if the soul were entirely immanent in it (whatever the latter alternative might exactly mean). If we allow ourselves to be dominated by the metaphor of a stream, as if our feelings, thoughts, and volitions simply flowed from a source in the past, then of course the contingency remains. But no arrest of the past-to-future current precludes its resumption from another direction. That *we*—ourselves as wholes—should cease to exist is not just a contingency. The very idea of death thus formed depends upon the prior negation of a real Ego, transcending our known time-order unidimensionally conceived.

And here we may notice a momentous discovery—for we cannot call it merely a theory—of Mr J. W. Dunne, that of the infinite regress of time-dimensions, which he claims to be the first scientific proof of immortality. This is not the place to dwell upon the significance of its positive contribution. The significance for us here is the breakdown, at the very start of the mathematical demonstration, of the *assumption* of unidimensional Time, an assumption that Bergson himself never detected as such, and which surely renders much that he has written on the subject obsolete. For it cannot possibly be maintained that the burden of proof rests upon the larger conception of Time—a conception, be it noted, that claims not to add to but to develop the simple idea—rather than upon the narrower.

Certainly, proof is needed; but, in a matter like this, we can draw no line between conceivability and actuality. To accept the mathematical validity of the dimensional series and yet to question whether any but one time-dimension belongs to factual and concrete reality is an absolutely impossible position to sustain. There is a widespread prejudice against such proofs. But their ideal, however arid they may seem to some, is to repair the very machinery of our thinking, and to disclose the defects in it to which many of our questions, not to mention the answers to them, are due.[1] That they are abstract and formal does not disqualify them as against an abstractly negative alternative: and such an alternative is the negation of a time-order dimensionally related to the series of sensations and events known to us as terminating in death. Such negation, or even doubt, is altogether different from the scrutiny rightly required for any empirical novelty that demands the revision of apparently established empirical conclusions.

Then, secondly, there is the problem of the body—the central point of conflict, fear and misgiving. Even if the difficulty is not regarded as fatal, it may seem rather a hopeless task so to extricate the idea of the soul from this implication of destructibility that intellectual conviction is absorbed into the absoluteness of spiritual belief. We make no use here of any but the ordinary naïve conception of Time. Apart from that limitation, the whole difficulty rests on the assumption that the visible earthly body is all the body that there is, or at least that its extension to unseen planes of material reality is mere hypothesis or unprovable occultism. But why so? *If* it can be maintained on other grounds that the personality survives, and that this involves some sort of corporeality, then surely the scope of the body must be understood accordingly. Is it not, after all, a gratuitous assumption that there is only one plane of material existence?

In short, whatever may be the discoveries of the future, they can never really call immortality into question, if we rightly understand its basis. They can only deprive us of modes of envisaging the soul in its relation to various phenomena or laws that have helped to keep alive our sense of its reality, and in so doing throw us back upon a more imageless and as it were ascetic thought. And that not

---

[1] Our own view is that this mathematical demonstration is but one side of a large re-adjustment of thought, which, fully carried through, would leave the idea of mortality (except in the religious context) meaningless. But we must not go farther into this.

because the being of the soul is aloofly and abstractly transcendent (that is not the true transcendence), but because it
is not in the least *committed* to any of the forms of explanation
that from time to time have helped us to realize it; because,
in the depth of the mystery that is behind both the spiritual
and the material, an infinity of possibility lies, which, if it
endangers our hypotheses, can also make good all our disappointments.

The mere negative idea of mortality is irrational. Nothing
in experience can, in the nature of the case, give any clue to
it. It can never escape from relativity, though it purports to
be absolute. Even a fainting-fit, for instance, we know only
as an event within experience, our own and that of others.
There is no experience of nonentity, or of entering upon
nonentity. The death of another is an event outside me. The
ultimate Ego does not, without begging the question, come
into the matter at all. We cannot even *conceive* the final arrest
of consciousness. We often think we can, because we can
arrest the *thought* of its continuance, which is quite a different
thing. Negative conclusions only push the problem—if we
call it a problem—farther back: it recedes *ad infinitum*. The
idea of immortality is related to that of our earthly life in
its entirety, our science with all the rest. The scope and
ontological significance of Science on the one hand and its
special place in the mind—general and individual—on the
other cannot be viewed apart.

Suppose we *posit* (simply) the reality of an eternal soul.
This, by hypothesis, is not separate from the mind that
operates on the earthly plane, and that concerns itself with
science and daily life: this mind belongs to it. Having once
clearly posed the question, let us ask ourselves: is it conceivable
that any development of investigation, and conclusions
therefrom on that plane, could discredit the reality of a
higher sphere of existence that by its meaning is related to
that plane in its totality and before its parts come into
question?

III

And now we come back again to death in its religious sense, to death as it stands over against the Gospel of Redemption—the "Second Death". (We are here outside the dimensional argument of Mr Dunne, as he himself would certainly affirm.)

As we have said before, death is, as such, annihilation. And this as a blank negative fact with no positive correlative is inconceivable. The truth, in our opinion, is that death is believed in because it is feared, not feared because it is believed in. The tendency to avoid that which causes death is a psychological phenomenon in line with the phenomena of organic existence. And it has a deep-lying metaphysical basis. It is the core of that essential self-reference which is implicit in all desire, just as self-consciousness is implicit in all thought.

In short, the idea of death is radical, yet irrational. But, in its religious aspect, the positive idea is before us. The very irrationality finds its place in the idea itself. We are in the region of the super-rational. We cannot conceive eternal death. But we do not need to conceive it. As the correlative of that final and central Revelation of one's own soul that the Gospel gives—as the depth disclosed by the Descent of God—we have experience of its meaning.

It is in this direction that the general idea of death—short of the revelation that completes the question in the very answering of it—tends, as we let its full meaning grow upon our minds. For a problem can only be clarified, not created, by its solution. But, at the long last, we have never faced the final issue till we have committed ourselves to that act and life of faith wherein alone the very central self—and implicitly the whole—passes through the absolute death—Christ's Death—into the absolute life.

Real death is the last supreme contradiction of thought and being. This, surely, is what remains when we have rejected all reductions and accommodations on the one hand

and all redundancies on the other. The Gospel has no private message of condemnation of its own. It simply lifts to the plane of absoluteness the universal truth that life seeks the maintenance of itself. Self-contradiction on the very ground of personality is the last supreme threat to the self-conscious being as such, the last negative become positive, the key to the final meaning of all avoidances and fears. The Gospel alone can speak coherently of absolute death, because it alone speaks to the absolute in man.

As eternal life is the fulfilment of man at his centre, so eternal death is the menace to that centre. It is a menace addressed to the innermost man, the soul within the soul. And, for this reason, its meaning is only explicit in the vision of the Creator, and in a crisis of decision made possible only by the Cross.

The sweeping assertion that the fear of Hell has never saved a soul is surely very untrue. But we have outgrown this crude interpretation of the backside of belief. Once we have realized that the true ultimate fear is radical, organic, metaphysical, natural in the deepest sense, we shall not need imported terrorisms, nor yet be drawn into vague speculations and guesses.

And notice how the *whole* idea of death is satisfied on this level. For all of it that is not seen in *antithesis* to the new life is absorbed and transmuted therein. Death to sin—death turned against itself—is only the other side of life unto God. But for this it might still be pleaded that death *has* a felt meaning, which cannot be set at rest by arguments against its abstract rationality. But its twofold character—of the enemy and of the servant—is satisfied in the revelation of the true Life. That is the meaning of the Cross and the Resurrection. The Cross is life because it is death: the Resurrection is death because it is life. Death has won the victory for us: it is the underside of the same victory won within us.

CHAPTER XI

SALVATION (II)

In the previous chapter we have tried so to ground our
idea of Salvation that it shall be free from compromises and
incomplete ideas, and broad enough to sustain all that must
be built upon it. Our quest, here as throughout, is no mere
theory, but the utmost logical reach of the New Testament
doctrine, as we most of us start from it together. In this
chapter it is our task to bring this fundamental idea into
relation with temporal conditions and the human will. We
have to consider: first, the claims made for human nature
antecedently to the Gospel; secondly, its response to the
Gospel; thirdly, its concurrent relation to Divine grace in the
course of the life of faith. However the phenomena overlap,
the essential distinctions will help us to arrange our ideas.

I

First, then, with regard to the moral assets which obviously
—it may seem—qualify the situation of dire need which
salvation meets. Does not the message address itself to these,
and are not the fruits of the new life continuous with them?
Our reply, whatever it may be, to this question must start
from our general conception of a consistent redemptional
theology. That the primary work of God's Spirit is not to
elicit but to confront, not to select but to re-create, is the
fundamental truth on God's side. And to this answers, on
man's side, the presentation, in a supreme act of faith, of his
whole self for pardon, deliverance, and transformation. Now
if we adhere closely to this idea of wholeness, we soon come
to see the corresponding conception of human need. That
conception excludes the theories which we have indicated
by the word "asset", and, on the other hand, it has no

suggestion of the old idea that human goodness is not really good "in the sight of God". But can we let go continuity? Does Christ need to do again in us what has been done already and survives? Certainly not, but He came to give *life*, and life is central and inclusive and presupposes death. We may speak of bringing back life to the almost dead by restoratives, but we do not really *bring* life; we assist its recovery. Christ really *brings* life. And there is no contradiction in affirming that that which is a live reality on the ethical plane has lost, by the Fall, its status in eternity. And the idea of salvation loses its completeness, and even its ultimate coherence, if we shirk its full correlative.

But here it must be added—otherwise we should be misunderstood—that this distinction of ideas is simply the *interpretation* of the facts that we see, not a clue to their classification. We cannot say "*This* is nature and *that* is grace." The grace of God is prevenient, and we know not how far back it may lie. But this does not stultify the distinction between nature and grace, the old creation and the new. Very far from it. The very meaning of the Gospel is involved—its centre of gravity, and the essence of its preacher's message. This note of detachment and transcendence re-asserts itself every time the Gospel confronts, in its own character, the hungry, the uneasy, or the callous soul. The man to whom Christianity is a *confluent* stream, that enlarges and purifies the current of his life-motives and highest thoughts, knows it as the noblest of religions, but he does not know it as Redemption.

Here, as throughout, if we only keep close to the idea of creation, as an unanalysable unit of thought, and resist the persistent urge to get behind it, the conception of natural righteousness takes its true place. The archetypal character of the Creator in relation to the universe of conscious beings is secured, but also the detachment and freedom of man, the possibility—which has become actuality—of his Fall, his possession still of divine qualities, which are really his, even in separation from his Creator. We can do without "immanence" here; a word which may easily mislead, even though the unexplained rejection of it may also mislead. The old simple doctrines of the Creation and the Fall make all clear and consistent. It is not a self-evident truth that, where divine qualities are, God is. We are only entitled to say that, where these are, God was. No logical necessity compels us, and no clear idea of creation and sin allows us, to regard the divine in man as anything but adjectival to the man. God is related to it, not as subject to predicate, but as Creator to creature. The Fall is unthinkable—sin is unthinkable—except as the alienation of the central man, at the focal point of his freewill, and therefore of his goodness. The goodness is certainly not transmuted into its opposite, nor does every vestige of it depart; but it is not God, nor part of God. And God, in Christ, re-creates us as wholes, because as wholes we have fallen, and because there is nothing in us that is not defiled by sin. It would be quite gratuitous to rest upon the faith that nothing good can perish. Goodness perishes continually in this life, in human characters. It is the tragedy of the Fall that it does. But a God immanent in the ruin would be a greater tragedy still.

II

The second point for consideration is the initial contact of the human will with the Divine saving will. It is in fact the question of conversion. Among us to whom the Divine *evangel* is the supreme and all-determining meaning of Christianity there are two points of view which it is instructive to set side by side. There is the view, characteristic of an old type, still vital but somewhat in the shadows (we ignore counterfeits and caricatures), that lays stress upon conversion as the one unique act of acceptance and self-surrender, dividing the preceding from the following years, and giving a distinct quality to the latter, besides the right to an assurance that liberates the soul for unselfish service. This does not mean an undiscriminating insistence upon so-called "sudden" conversion. The obvious fact that conversion may be implicit rather than explicit (these are the right words) is not necessarily overlooked. There is childhood to be considered, and many believing people, whose wills are surely converted, do not even accept any real doctrine of conversion at all. But it is the explicit event that gives the key to its meaning.

The outstanding and pronounced example of the other type is the Barthian school. The line is drawn here, not *across* the biographical line, but longitudinally. Or, to put it in another way, the line is a razor-edge, and the soul lives in the tension between judgement and salvation.

These two views, we believe, qualify, but do not entirely contradict, one another. We have already commented on the inadequacy of the Barthian conception of faith. Faith must be regarded as comprehensive as well as punctual, in its relation to our life-history, if the idea of it is to be consistently worked out. But, on the other hand, we have strongly adhered to their conception of direct volitional faith, as against any confusion of it with opinion or experience. The object of the Christian's faith is not the faith itself, but the love of God in the Cross. His assurance, however, does not live only in the instant of its renewal. If it persists beyond the punctual act of faith, it does not therefore become illicit, or a mere venture of unauthorized opinion. The older view stands for continuity, and that with no intention to deny the directly Godward orientation of faith. Nor is it wrong in the significance it attaches to genuine explicit conversion. For, if the principle of crisis is accepted as a pivotal idea in our theology, we should not overlook the outstanding place that real conversion takes among types of crisis. It is, after all, the least inadequate of the temporal phenomena of the act of faith. And yet we do not think that entire justice has always been done by preachers of this type to the truth in the other view. The primary thing to preach is not conversion but the Gospel. And it has not been by any means an unknown thing for the Gospel itself to be forgotten by the Gospel preacher in his pre-occupation with the appeal for self-surrender.

III

Thirdly, we come to the implication of the human will in the claims and experiences of the daily life. This is the sphere in which *law*, within the consecrated life, is still, *mutatis mutandis*, relevant; and therewith conflict, confusion, delayed victory; menace on the one hand, compromise on the other.

For, obviously, we are not yet governed completely by the love to God and man, by the purity of heart, by the perfect spirit of truth, that the new life imparts. And there is no neutral or common territory between law and grace. Even the law of Christ is still law. And, on the other hand, the Gospel, as Brunner truly says, is in the indicative tense, not in the imperative. This inner secret of the faith is cheaply purchased even by the sharper antithesis in which, by consequence, the law, in all its forms, stands out against the Gospel, and the sense of its solemn presence whenever our eyes are turned away from the Cross. It is easy to say that God is our loving Father, and that, even as Lawgiver, we need not dread Him. But, if we no longer think it "a fearful thing to fall into the hands of the living God", it is certainly a fearful thing to fall out of them. And the faith that we shall not fall out of them is stultified when we will to disobey. For obedience is implicated in that faith.

Still, however, the fact remains that the realities and necessities of the Christian life are not all reducible to pure imperative and pure grace. We have called attention at an earlier stage to the irrationalism at the heart of Ethics, to the lack of that very lucidity and coherence that its own meaning demands. And it is just the same when the law of right and wrong becomes to us the law of God and Christ. For indeed

God *is* not law, as He is holiness and love. This is the sphere of moral judgement, of spiritual culture, of Divine *assistance*, the sphere of relativity and Time. Here it is that we have to fight self-deception and weakness; none the less though at the long last the decisive weapon is faith.

But the imperative is not always law: it is also particular *command*. This relieves the pressure. Its ideal is achieved if the very voice from Sinai becomes the voice behind us saying "This is the way: walk ye in it": when the law itself breaks up among the several individuals, and among the several occasions of those individuals' lives. Of course, so long as we must use the word "command" the imperative is not yet entirely transformed into an inspired spontaneity. But here at least is a frontier-line between law and grace, which we shall do well to understand.

"Guidance" is in the air just now. It has to meet a very serious objection: that we are apt to take as the voice of God what is in fact only a voice from another part of ourselves. This objection should be faced squarely, for not merely is it a criticism, sound or unsound, of a particular religious practice: it opens the way to conclusions relevant to our immediate subject. Self *ought* to rule self, if the ruling self knows itself as ruled. Divine guidance does not, in all cases, supersede our own judgement—even moral judgement—or guarantee its infallibility. But the Spirit-guided life *as a whole*—the very fact of its being—is the fruit of a union, at the hidden centre, of the human will with the Divine, where, in principle and in promise, the law is already fulfilled and transcended. This consideration relieves the paradox of a clash between the general and the particular will of God, the paradox of an inward imperative to do what is in itself wrong. The anomaly of split duty still remains, for it is part of the anomalous condition introduced by sin, but we understand it as such better. The severance of the moral imperative into two sometimes incompatible halves calls our attention to the organic disease of human nature, which can only be met by action from outside even the healthiest and best elements of the affected subject, as is the action of the physician.

Part of the aim of the renewed will is to reduce this anomaly to a minimum, that is, to seek to know the will of God. This very quest itself presupposes the supreme assent to the supreme meaning of that will. On this basis the personal commandment takes control. It is the *tertium quid* between the law as *presupposed* by the Gospel and the law as transcended and absorbed by it. But to hear the Divine voice unambiguously, undistracted by counter-voices within and without, is the ideal, not the starting-point. Meanwhile faith looks above even the conflict in which its own relative and impeded action is the decisive factor, to the Divine victory of the Resurrection.

We often speak—as we must—of God's "help", or of His "strength" imparted to us. These terms are relative to the *particular* needs of our souls. They are applicable to the Christian life regarded discursively, not in direct relation to the ultimate issue. Only in respect of our victories regarded severally, not of salvation as such, does God's grace play this subsidiary part. It is sometimes said that God saves us by giving us the power—through self-sacrifice—to save ourselves. But this is only a subtle form of Synergism. For the human will is thus regarded as acting—however previously enabled—on its own basis, and the results as, even at the last analysis, its own achievement. The enabling is an external pre-condition. Self-salvation by the enabling of grace is not essentially different from self-salvation by the enabling of creation.

Parallel considerations apply to merit. The valuation of human merit corresponds to the untrusting diffidence that is apt to accompany the sense of demerit. It is extraordinary to hear it said that one ought not, as a matter of self-respect, to desire a heaven that one has not earned. We are tempted to ask those who say such things whether they would refuse a legacy. But we do very seriously maintain that we have no right to set up our own little superiorities against God's mercy, even on an hypothesis that we reject. At the bottom of this false dignity lies unbelief. To say in effect that *if* God gave, we should decline, is neither rational nor reverent. And, besides, "heaven" includes by definition spiritual transformation, and it seems very odd indeed to say that we would not be good too soon even if we had the chance.

Assuredly, we can find support for such types of teaching in the New Testament, if we refuse to recognize the difference of strata in it, the greater concreteness and finality of some elements than of others. But then we might as well refuse all advance from the crudest *primâ facie* conception of the Judgement by works. It is only if we force them on to the plane of the absolute Gospel that they contradict it. Surely the final truths in the New Testament, if it is indeed revelation, are those which most need revealing—those which point us most paradoxically, and without qualification, to the Divine "foolishness" of the Cross and the Ascension—the mysteries that confront us, even at our intellectual and spiritual best, from without and above.

But, granted that the Divine saving Act is, on the one side, forgiveness, and, on the other, the gift of a new heart and a new will, there is still a question to be asked. Are we to regard the motives and powers of the new life simply as supernatural and, as it were, super-psychological? Or are they the natural and inevitable result of a new situation, a new vision, a new direction of mind and life? We preserve the truth in both alternatives if we say that they are the natural and inevitable result of the one supernatural gift of the new life with its new vision and orientation. That God saves us by a direct appeal to our emotions is an idea entirely outside our pale. Subjectivist theories of salvation are the death of all definite Christianity. But to try to focus the objective is a very different matter. And if, indeed, the regenerative act of God is re-*creative*, this should not be difficult. The individual man, the simple unit of creation, is the logical prius of all that he is and does. So is he also, in his undivided wholeness, the unit of re-creation. The new subjective orientation is itself *given*, that is, supernatural.

The ethical side of salvation is, of course, expressed in feelings, impulses, and settled dispositions. These are neither infused nor elicited. But each of these views, wrong in itself, contains an element corrective of the other.

As to infusion. If salvation is indeed the raising of fallen man—man whom God has created in His own image—it is clear that, when raised, he will be—or begin to become—the true man of God's original design. His virtues will not be infused: they will spring to life within the organism of the "new creature", in the soil of the Kingdom of God. But this means also that they are not elicited from any inherited potentialities. For, if so, we do not need life, but stimulation. As against both these opposite errors, we set the Act—only thinkable as His whose it is—of the Creator-Redeemer. The idea of infusion is true in so far as it asserts objectivity, initiation, and the approach from without. The rival idea, on the other hand, on the face of it, preserves the integrity of the creative plan. But neither is true to the inclusiveness of spiritual death, nor its correlative, the centrality of the new life.

Renewing grace does not, then, act in a crudely miraculous manner upon the old character, nor yet, as it were, overtake it from the creative spring *behind*. It is invasive, but at the centre. Its particular effects, once produced, fall under the laws of our psychic nature. The phenomena of auto-suggestion, sublimation, and so forth, here play an important part. They cut us off from the poor resources of a discursive supernaturalism, and drive us in toward the blank at the centre where we call for and find God. Has not Jung declared that none of his psychopathic patients has been truly cured in the long run without religion? And yet, if we were to take even this as the last word, we should be making religion just a cure among cures, even though the final and essential cure. We could not just adopt religion, so recommended, as a cure, as we might follow a doctor's prescription. It is God who saves; and religion itself, like virtue—considered as *ours* —may even be an obstacle to grace.

The main point upon which it is necessary to insist is simply this: transcendent and external action, wrought *upon* us, yet upon what is most internal in us, is the key to the meaning of all that God does for us. If we think of its working discursively, its transcendence does not so plainly appear: and that is because it enters pre-existing channels, to expand or divert them, or makes natural channels of its own. Our nature, when God has acted upon it, shows marks of His action. But He acts upon the innermost in us, wherein lies the secret, not of our resources, but of our bankruptcy.

But the point of supernatural impact on the several occasions, clearly differentiated, remains not only empirically obscure, but, in the nature of the case, indiscoverable. The one absolute focus is the Cross. Subjective experiences can find no stable reference-point or foothold except here. It is the same in our use of the Sacraments. Here we have objective centres of presentation and opportunity, distributed in time and space. But, just because the whole creed is focused *by* them, they themselves cannot be the focus. They are transparent. The faith they demand and the experience they create look behind and above them.

What we have just said should help us to see that a full belief in the activity of a transcendent God does not depend upon a direct and infallible apprehension of it on particular occasions. The central redemptive Act is not only historical but super-historical. It embraces, not indeed the race in the abstract, but the concrete reality of living men and women throughout the ages, barring only the recalcitrance of freewill. It guarantees the Divine *side* of all the relevant phenomena of life, though their outlines, even so regarded, remain blurred in the mists of the time-plane.

At the present day it should not be hard to make real to

ourselves the thought of a supreme *Object* which is, in itself, the one necessary factor for the renewing of character and life. Evil impulses may be sublimated into healthy channels, when a new centre of interest and attention is afforded. (It is not Rationalism to refuse to cling to *old* difficulties merely for the sake of a directly supernatural solution.) Our reaction to life and the world depends on the light in which we see them. Hort has a profound saying to the effect that all thoughts that are base, cruel, anti-social, are first of all untrue. And the old *mechanism* of the ideal life is in us, as God's creatures, already. Redemption is the *second* act of Ezekiel's vision. The dry bones are articulated. What is needed is the Life. And the Light is the Life. "We shall be like Him, *for* we shall see Him as He is."

But, if the Light is the Life, no less the Life is the Light. This is absolutely vital, for nothing could be farther from our intention than to reduce the new life to the subjective influences of the reminiscences of a wonderful Man. God's Revelation is not only the giving of the Object, but the giving of the eyesight. And that means nothing less than the raising from the dead. And the saving Act—with the pardon and the promise within it—is itself the primary thing that it gives us the sight to see.

But is this not to attach to mystic experience an importance far exceeding anything that the majority of us can perceive in our own minds? When we try to think of our thought of God, we often see little or nothing; no more perhaps than what someone has described from his own experience, "a sort of oblong blur". But this is not thinking of *God*. The direct vision of God, however, does not guarantee a vision of the vision. Our most central knowledge of God may elude our reflection, but it may yet be the pivot of our thoughts. That our reflection is thus out of gear with the higher immediacy is the provisional and anomalous situation which awaits the taking up of Time into Eternity.

CHAPTER XII

THE ATONEMENT (I)

We use this term in the sense in which it is ordinarily used, however abandoned in our theories. That is to say, we apply it, not to the Divine *methods* of salvation—the economy of grace—but to the presupposition that lies behind all this, the ethical meaning of the event of Redemption as an event; in other words, to the rationale of Divine forgiveness, its intrinsic character as expressed in act. Not to distinguish between these aspects is to oscillate between confusing and separating them. So, on the other hand, following our guiding principle *Distinguish to unite*, we shall endeavour to preserve, as it appears to us, the essential inter-dependence of these two aspects of truth within the inclusive idea of Redemption.

The implications of the meaning of forgiveness—that is, the complete meaning of complete forgiveness—should lead us to the very heart of the idea of the Atonement. That is what we may look for if we seek so to understand that meaning that the very core of it does not escape us (no unnecessary caution), and also that it may be seen to bear that quality of absoluteness, infinity, and ideal fulfilment that belongs to it as directly attributed to the transcendent personality of God. The following points should guide us on our road.

First, forgiveness is personal, or super-personal, not forensic or governmental. Sin, as we have seen, is committed against God solely and directly. The cancellation of guilt at the psychological moment—any restoration of the sinner on grounds of subjective qualification—is not in itself forgiveness at all. The frequent *association* of all this with elements of sympathy and human feeling obscures for us that otherwise obvious truth; and, at the same time, we are inclined to drop personal—that is, true—forgiveness more or less out of sight, because it seems to presuppose a personal conception of penalty, unworthy of God. We allude to this difficulty at once, that it may not seem that we are not alive to it, but reserve our answer for the moment.

The second and third essentials are complementary one to the other. The second, which is obvious, is this: to forgive is of the very essence of the Divine nature. Human forgiveness, man being imperfect, may be unpredictable. Divine forgiveness is not, *in that sense*, unpredictable.

But, thirdly, in another sense, it is. It is included in the Divine nature, but the Divine nature receives, for us, its true expression in an empirical Fact, the Cross. It is therefore a paradox, as the Cross is a paradox. It may be said, indeed, that the greatest forgiver is one who forgives spontaneously, without inward change, and that the greatest forgiveness would be expected from him. But there remains the paradox of his very existence; and this shines forth on any particular great occasion of his forgiveness, even though it may involve no mental change, or even act, on his part; even though the injurer may, as it were, fall into the forgiveness in falling into the sin. But forgiveness is not just the negative fact that God is above human resentments. That is a paradox in man, but not in God. There must be something therefore in God, and not hidden from our finite minds, that makes it as such intelligible.

This brings us to our fourth point. Forgiveness in man —and *mutatis mutandis* in God—cannot arise from a single emotion or sentiment. If it is positive at all, if it is more than simply not resenting, it implies a certain tension between two elements, *one* of which we may call love, in the character of the forgiving subject. We do not, in all particular cases, assume such tension to be operative: we may admire the forgiver for its very absence: but the implication of it is at the root of the idea; and only where it is in some way present is the essential meaning of forgiveness fully exemplified. In the highest cases of human forgiveness the impulse that the love-impulse overcomes is not what we should call absolutely bad. But it is some sort of egoistic urge which would inhibit more or less our acts or feelings of kindness, or the restoration of friendship. Now we have to ask: How does it stand in the case of infinite and perfect Being?

For there is no moral deficiency in God Himself; and there could be no possible conflict of motives, or conceivable parting of the ways, in the course of His action. Our human infirmities and our need to choose between alternatives seem to bar the application of what we have said to God Himself, and thus to make His forgiveness, taken seriously as such, hard to understand. What is there in God, answering to undivine qualities in man, that forms the counter-principle to love, and thus gives a meaning to *His* forgiveness?

The idea of the Divine *holiness* has already come before us, and we have tried to show how in four manners it has been explained away by those who do not think of directly denying it. We have said that holiness and love are one just because they are one in God, not because of any possibility of fusing the two ideas. There they mutually draw together, and this synthesis is what we call the Atonement. There is indeed no *actual* tension between holiness and love in God Himself; but there *is* a tension, insoluble by pure reason, in our thought about Him; and this tension sets that final question to which the revelation of the Cross alone can give the answer.

And this answer is not separable from the Fact: not just proved or symbolized by it, but *in* it. Even the bare historical fact is not symbol or drama or proof. It is *contact*. Definite happening within the time-order—however criticism may deal with the records—is necessary to that stark externality that meets the whole man, reason and all, as his and its radical salvation.

Holiness, then, plays that part in our conception of the

Atonement that is played by the elements other than love in the man who forgives. And this correspondence, notwithstanding all the difference, is surely not far to seek. The violated holiness is, as we have seen, the very Godhead of God. In God this motive does not impinge upon infinite love: the Cross is not an afterthought. That holiness and love are thus united in one expression only means that *God* loves. To say that God *is* Love certainly does not supersede the simple proposition that God loves, and so does not answer the question "Who and what is the One who loves?"

Then as to alternatives of action. We do not need to think of God as at the parting of the ways—and cannot, just for the reason that in Him perfect freedom is realized. In God freedom does not rest upon the possibility of alternatives, but upon the absoluteness of His Being. It is easy so to misapprehend absolute Being that the very attribute of perfect freedom, which itself demands, is stultified. It is only in the absolute *God*, directly apprehended as such—the freely self-giving Absolute, antecedent to all philosophy—that the true idea of pure freedom is given to us, not in the philosophic Absolute conceived as God.

The upshot of this is that we must not spoil our sense of the meaning of Divine forgiveness, or atonement, by misgivings about alternative possibilities unworthy of God. It does not presuppose even the thinkableness of non-forgiveness. But it does mean that, in our understanding of it, the idea of love must interact with another element in the idea of the Divine. What is behind that interaction is not a higher category, but the undivided reality of God Himself, known only in His self-revelation.

If holiness and love are to be seen united in action, the Act must be such as to exhibit love under conditions that exhibit holiness. How the Divine Act meets this requisite is a question that we shall answer by no new theory; indeed, no theory at all. The answer lies to hand for all who can accept the doctrinal context to which it belongs.

There is another aspect of the matter that may be fittingly introduced here. That is, the relation of forgiveness to *Repentance*. It is noticeable that our Lord clearly associates the duty of forgiveness with repentance on the part of the injurer. To a certain extent we can understand this. Personal forgiveness—which is forgiveness proper—may not be the only demand made by the situation. There is the claim of moral law, which, between man and man, while men are sinful, cannot be wholly superseded or wholly depersonalized. But, if forgiveness is essentially personal, such considerations do not qualify it in its essence. There is such a thing as human forgiveness without repentance, and its moral value, especially in a sensitive nature, no one would deny. It may, of course, be made easier by characteristics that are in themselves weaknesses rather than otherwise. It may, on the other hand, be a supreme moral achievement. And it completes the meaning of forgiveness. For imperfection in repentance is simply imperfect detachment from the evil mind in us that did the wrong, from which if we were wholly detached, there would not be anything left to pardon. Complete repentance would even give a *right* to pardon, which is self-contradictory. As to the Divine pardon, it is certainly based upon this principle. Christ died for us "while we were yet sinners".

However, we do usually distinguish between the Atonement, as the basal act, and the forgiveness of the individual, which takes place upon repentance. Can this be squared with our present endeavour to see in the Atonement the perfected idea of forgiveness?

It seems clear that, nevertheless, the full idea of forgiveness *is* present in that of Atonement. We have seen that the Atonement answers *mutatis mutandis* to the human act of forgiveness, considered as the inward act of the forgiving subject; and it certainly finds expression limited only by freewill, that is, by the inherent impossibility of forcing reformation upon anybody. Forgiveness, unlike reconciliation, is unilateral, and is certainly not limited in itself by anything outside itself that thwarts its *action*—not even by lack of response, which only enhances it. The initial urge to repentance and the acceptance of it are alike God's act, and therefore one act, broken only by the opposition of human freewill. We naturally use the term forgiveness when we speak of God's acceptance of repentance. But, none the less, though not coercive, it is prevenient. It is part of the one temporal-eternal Act that embraces all and each. It is neither separate nor divided; for the Cross is the forgiveness of the concrete existential human race: therefore of each individual sooner or later, subject only to the veto—albeit the tacit veto—of his will. In this matter the Divine Act is different from the human.

Lastly, we have so far regarded forgiveness in its aspect as an inward quality or act. Even as actively expressed, it has come before us as the solution of what in our thought is a tension, and which, if it were not a tension there, would be a tension within the nature of God Himself. We have now to ask what the act in itself is. In man forgiveness may be purely inward, for there may be no opportunity of giving it even verbal expression. But potentially—and, when possible, necessarily—it acts. Its impulse is twofold: to benevolent action and to restored friendship or communion. In God these are both satisfied by the taking of us into His inner presence, from which sin, by its very meaning, has excluded us, and by the grace and the promise which this comprises. The pardoning act is simply the whole act of salvation, in its eternal completeness. For salvation, as we know it now in face of its subjective problems and crises, is gradual: pardon is complete or nothing.

While, then, God does not forgive us in an act of change within Himself, he does forgive us in a manward act. And —once more—the Act is one, not many. It is radical, in the race as in the individual, even as sin is radical, and perfect, as God is perfect. Specific and recurrent pardon gives us but glimpses of its meaning, just as actual sins give us but glimpses of the meaning of sin.

We have now reached our doctrine of the Atonement. We have tried to indicate that the Death of Christ is not just a condition, presenting a problem, of God's forgiveness, but, with all its historicity, an integral element in that idea. This conclusion has been arrived at by a study of forgiveness in itself, in that ideal form that it presents on the level of the eternal and the divine, and by an attempt to understand thereby precisely what transformation and enhancement the idea undergoes when seen in this light. We are now at the heart of the Christian creed.

CHAPTER XIII

THE ATONEMENT (II)

We may say at the outset of this chapter that the view of Atonement that belongs—and alone belongs—to the main standpoint of this book is that called the "classic view" by the Swedish writer of a notable work *Christus Victor*. The writer, Dr Aulén, who himself accepts it, distinguishes it sharply as one of three broad conceptions of the Atonement. Of the other two, one is the Abelardian, also called—in the teeth of protest—the subjective. And then there is what he calls the "Latin", and this includes a number of theories, conservative and modern, but all characterized by the postulate, in some form, of an *active*, or at least positive, part played by the humanity of Christ in the Atonement, such as representation, universal manhood, and the strange modern theory of the Perfect Penitent. This type includes Anselm, the medievalists generally, and the Reformers, except Luther. The third, which he calls the classical, and which, he maintains, is the doctrine of the New Testament and also of the earlier Fathers and of Luther, simply accepts the Atonement as the direct undivided act of God, including Christ in His *Divine* nature. The human nature is the medium or instrument, not the agent or co-agent. This stands in contrast to the double, or broken, act implied by the interposition of a Man-offered Sacrifice or the plea of perfect human righteousness. The classic type has, in general, been too obvious to be noticed, and has suffered more from neglect than from attack. But what if that which we have taken as the raw material of our theories is really God's own theory?

It is from no disrespect to those who have defended the Abelardian theory that we do not consider its claims. Its affirmations are too plainly inadequate to our central thesis, and its negations are met by the main line of thought throughout these pages. But a brief consideration of the Latin type will merge into an exposition of the classic, as we understand and apply it.

I

We cordially recognize the insistence on objectivity and the reverence for the Law that are the outstanding marks of this type, and the far greater justice done by it to the main idea of Redemption than by advanced Liberalism. But we believe that it deals in sophistication and redundancy, and that redundancy in theology is always also corrosive negation.

The logic of a truly consistent Anti-Pelagianism must lead us in the end to affirm that the human race did not and cannot save itself, even in the Person of Christ. It is not an entity, and the Incarnation could not make it one—certainly not in such a sense as to supersede, even for the moment, the personal units of which it consists. Even if we thought of it as being a definite whole, we should have to bear in mind a remark of Rashdall's, made in another connection, but useful in many; namely, that, though it is true that the whole is more than the sum of its parts, it must not be forgotten that it *is* the sum of its parts. The volition of the Saviour cannot stand, even provisionally, for that of men, regarded—as they must be regarded—severally. If this is supposed, a dilemma results. The closer we connect, in our thought, the human race with the concrete Person of Christ, by so much the more do we view it in abstraction from the individual persons who are the objects of His saving act: and, alternatively, the more consistently we see the race in *them*, the more are we compelled to think of Him as one—albeit supreme—individual among them. And neither alternative will bear the weight of the theory. Whether we adhere to some mystical idea of recapitulation or are content with simple representation, we are equally unable to carry our meaning through. Sin is personal: the race-as-a-whole, as we have said of race sinfulness, is an abstraction. In any case, it cannot act in one person, not even that of the Son of Man, and its representation by the Sinless would be misrepresentation.

Here we may expect to be met with the idea of anticipatory representation. Christ is qualified to represent men, it is said, because the perfecting of the race *will* through Him be carried out in existential reality. Undoubtedly, this future reference is implied in the fact of the Atonement. Also it does not conflict with what we have said about the race and the individual, even if we reject universalism. That the race consists of individuals does not mean that the totality of them, or any inner circle of the "elect", makes up its completeness, only that everyone that is born in it is a necessary recipient of what the race receives, barring the veto—somewhere and somehow—of his freewill. But this future reference does not make valid any theory of anticipatory *representation*. We may, with the Abelardians, sweep away the entire idea of an objective Sacrifice directly related to forgiveness (and the Latin theories give some plausibility to the rejection); but, if we admit it at all, we cannot possibly explain it in terms of its result. Salvation presupposes God's knowledge that man is salvable, but God would know this just the same without representation. If forgiveness requires a *ground*, that ground must be some present concrete actuality, not the anticipation of what will be after its own acceptance. Teaching of this type cannot be dissociated from the protean Pelagianism of our hearts. The abstract realism, or the unreal formalism, of its view of the race must in the long run tend, by compensation, to leave the individual detached and semi-independent.

II

Surely the essential idea of the Divine Sacrifice, as we find it in the New Testament, and as the logic of the Gospel requires, is simple enough. That it is offered *by* God *to* God is no greater mystery than that of the Incarnation and the Trinity. What we see here is simply the indivisible and ineffable perfection of Deity manifested *in terms of* human obedience and self-abnegation. The Eternal Sonship behind this secures its transcendence of the human medium.

Referring to the preceding chapter, we find the actual emergence of the idea of sacrifice—applicable to God Himself—from the simple idea of forgiveness. Divine forgiveness requires no ground outside itself and its own definition. The great error of the theory rightly or wrongly called subjective is not that it denies such ground, but that its own conception of Divine forgiveness has no ground. By its virtual denial of the *category* of holiness, it undermines the divine character of perfect love, and also the very meaning of forgiveness, as embodied in *a forgiving*. And even the completeness of the forgiveness, which it especially undertakes to guard, is, as Aulén points out, qualified when it is said that God forgives on the condition of repentance: for the world did not repent first. The condition of forgiveness—that is, sacrifice—must be internal to the very meaning of forgiveness. This meaning must be such as to render intelligible God's reconciliation to man, forgiveness being what it is and God being what He is. And it all amounts to this: that, if we are to bring these two ideas together, we must see the Divine love as conditioned, not only externally—by the situation it meets—but within the Forgiver. In the Cross we see the tension between holiness and love, and its removal. Or, more truly, we see what would have been a tension, but for the Cross. If it be said that there *could* be no such tension, that is true; but neither could God have done anything but what He has done. No co-operation, in any form, of the beneficiary race is necessary

or conceivable. Even man's response is an *acceptance*,
and also the creation, of the grace to which he responds.

How this is so appears now immediately, and needs no
theory. That Holiness and Righteousness are satisfied in the
self-sacrifice of God Himself: that Sin has reacted as it has
upon God in His very condemnation of it—so reacted by
His own choice—satisfies utterly and entirely the meaning
of Sin on the one hand and of Holiness on the other. This is,
in fact, almost a commonplace, but it is kept in the background by two tendencies of thought: that which is unaffected
by the question that it answers, and that which looks, in
various ways, for a human share in the solution.

The Divine Sacrifice stands behind and beneath all Christian
sacrifice. The latter is not continuous with it, but its consequence and creation. St Paul, it is true, stepping outside
the ordinary lines of his thinking, alludes to his own sufferings
as "filling up that which was lacking" in those of Christ.
If we accept sentiment *as* such, and discard all mystical
theorizing based upon it, we shall find in such a passage
nothing that does not rest directly upon the simple facts.
When all is said about the "finished work" (and how closely
we are holding to that idea needs not to be insisted on), there
remains the fact that Christ's work and sufferings were also
—from another point of view—a beginning. They were the
beginning of a temporal process, the process of gathering
and incorporating a redeemed humanity into Himself around
the nucleus of the one human Body that He assumed. And
that process included His own *human* ministry. And, as all
Christian service is continuous with His ministerial service
here on earth, so are the sufferings that attend it. St Paul
does not attach a vague mystical value to suffering regarded
ex parte ante. He does not think of himself as a joint fulfiller
with his Lord of some mysterious "law" of the universe.
Painful duties, present and expected, were to him a concrete
given reality, empirically assigned to him as a particular
individual, as to others in their measure, according to circum-

stance and the wisdom of God. *Given* the sufferings, endured or expected, they become solid with those of Christ, and supplement them, not intensively but extensively: not at that absolute centre where atonement lies: not where the infinite value of the Divine self-giving admits of no increment or completion: but at the frontier where the Kingdom of God still faces the adverse powers and the unfinished task.

That the human sufferings of Christ were also, because of the unity of His Person, Divine sufferings does not, to our mind, involve any form of Patripassianism. It does not even follow that, because His Incarnation and Death expressed the perfect love and compassion of the Godhead, we must regard suffering, in God—apart from the humanity—as involved in His compassion—which is a moot point. There is no need, however, to discuss it here.

To conclude our remarks upon the Sacrifice. What has been said is quite consistent with the indubitable fact that it was, in one aspect, a sacrifice offered by man to God. It had the psychological and ethical content of humanly offered sacrifice. But by *a* Man. What we are obliged to deny is that, so regarded, it functioned in the Godward *atoning* Act. As atonement, it was a purely Divine act, including, as it did, the *becoming* Man. We must distinguish between the Sacrifice as the Divine climax of the Divine Act of Incarnation and the same as the climax of human victory and self-surrender. In the latter, narrower, aspect it was certainly human, but not the act of the race performed in Christ or of Christ as representing the race. It was an individual act, not super-individual. God's self-identification with humanity, as a unit within it, clearly involved such a sacrifice; for, as it was the free act of God, so it was a free act also in terms of human nature, under the conditions of the Incarnation, and, as such, the self-sacrifice of the human Christ to God. Thus the acceptance of it was not the acceptance of mankind, but of the "Forerunner" into the central place where He could be the Saviour of Mankind.

III

We need not say much about those various terms associated with the doctrine of the Atonement, such as wrath, propitiation, and so forth, which prove a stumbling-block to so many. These are exemplified and understood in the relations between man and man. They are applied to our relations to God in various manners and with varying degrees of softening and apology. Or they are discarded, and the vain attempt is made to make love cover everything. It is perfectly clear that the general understanding of the Atonement—however human and erroneous—sets it in the light of an answer to problems of mind and heart that have been more or less formulated in harsher terms. It is of little use to explain these problems and misgivings as due to the ignorance, blindness, and base anthropomorphisms that corrupt religion. They could form no connection, however illicit, with its central ideas and higher experiences, if there were nothing in these that corresponded with something in them. But, once we have secured our standpoint, this becomes more a question of terminology than anything else. Our central belief will not be built on these terms, but will itself separate out —however inarticulately—the truth from the falsity in them. And here comes in the ethico-religious value of Otto's study of the idea of the Holy. It releases and focalizes that essentially unique and permanent element in our thought of Sin and Atonement, which cannot be expressed adequately or without alloy in terms not taken from the vocabulary of religion.

There is, however, one idea of wider import that cannot be quite passed over, a centre of controversy that is not purely theological. It is often debated whether or no punishment is retributive. Now it would seem that, if it is ever correct to condemn any particular punishment as unjust, there must be some punishment which—apart from being otherwise demanded—is *just*. It might indeed be maintained that the justice is only negative, and does not involve any retributive character in punishment. But still why is it said that some punishment is wrong because it is *not* just? Can it be said that injustice is a positive quality in punishment, but that justice is not? It is true that forgiveness of real sin would not be unjust. Retribution need not be understood as a moral duty: but it may still be an implication of the moral consciousness. We have seen previously that the claims of duty cannot retain their *imperative* character if they depend entirely upon moral *appeal*. Even the most rigid follower of pure duty, who scorns consequences, exhibits this implication. For such a nature treats self as if it were another: self becomes the hard master of self.

When we come to Theology, we see how the essential truth of the idea is sifted out. Retribution is absorbed in the atoning Death. But how much of its meaning can we indicate as *presupposed* by the message of the Atonement? Two points seem clear. First, in theology, the centre of gravity is shifted from the question as it applies to the several acts and occasions of human punishment to the broad relation between Good and Evil; and this in itself lightens the pressure of the problem. Secondly, this final solution seems to favour —paradoxically perhaps—the Greek rather than the Hebrew conception of retribution, so far as the former regarded it more as impersonal, even though personified, than as a moral quality in a personal God. It is, of course, the Hebrew idea that is the real introduction, intrinsically as historically, to the Gospel. Retribution had to be conceived in personal terms, even at the cost of alloy, before it could be assimilated by the personal Theism consummated and refined in the Gospel. But to assimilate is to supersede. It is just the idea that is *not* transmuted that retains a certain validity of its own to the end. If so, we may avail ourselves of the impersonal conception of Retribution when we are thinking on the lower plane.

IV

But there is another vital aspect of the Christian message that the classic doctrine brings into strong relief, and, we venture to say, alone establishes in its true setting. It is that of the Divine *Victory* over Evil. Let us note carefully the connection with the preceding.

The doctrine of the one specific Act of God does not, like other theories, divide human nature. It preserves the unity of man, as it does the unity of God. Humanity does not save humanity, nor does God simply side with the best in humanity against the worst. This applies alike to the race and to the individual. Whatever relative truth there is in this latter idea, it is subject to the basal truth of the one consummate Act. The *dividedness itself* is the sinful condition, and so *constitutes the primary situation with which Redemption is confronted.* As God is one, so was man one till he lay broken at the feet of God. That the higher in man is separated from the lower, and conflicts with it, is significant of a presence of sin that embraces both. Here we have the key alike to racial Redemption and to individual need and salvation. That is the first link in the connection.

The second follows inevitably. We cannot consistently think of God as, in the unity of His action, confronting man in the broken unity of his nature without the emergence into clear-cut visibility of a third factor in the situation. That is the Power from which man has to be delivered, the Enemy that occasions the descent to Death of the Omnipotent, the *objective evil principle,* however exactly conceived. It is just because Sin, as seen from this standpoint, is so inward and central to man, while yet at the same time he is God's creature and not of evil essence, that it must be regarded as also in some sense outside, possessing and encompassing him. And again, on God's side, we cannot give a stable place in our minds to the thought of an explicit interventional Act—as distinguished from various immanental theories—except as against a counter-principle, somehow transcending man.

The question wherein the objectivity of Sin is embodied is not absolutely precluded, but the answer is a corollary. It can only be answered—so far as we can see—by finding what the *minimal* postulate is that the case itself requires. We thus exclude all speculation, and the reproach of "mythology" becomes utterly unfair. *If*, for instance, the literal idea of a personal Devil is required by the general conception, we can accept the idea just in such a form as it *is* required, and any mythological dressing is distinguished as such. In all ultimate theological thinking we can always, as it were, pull up short, when the abyss of mystery confronts us disconcertingly in the middle of our path. Our very submission to Revelation gives the charter of a new freedom in the handling of the instruments of thought.

Thus we have disclaimed the rounded-off concepts of a theory. If to those accustomed to rationalistic modes of thinking the classic view seems an unfinished, and probably unfinishable, conception, we can only say that this is in our eyes one of its supreme merits. We cannot arrive at any sound idea of the unity of reason with religious faith unless they interlock, and they cannot interlock if reason makes closed theories on the very frontier, any more than if faith, on its side, shuns contact with it. Of course the old phraseology may call for restatement. We can put the matter more philosophically when required; but this means simply to reduce it to its really necessary terms, and to explain it in relation to the other contents of our minds. But to explain, in this sense, is very different from the common method of explaining away.

An instance of the latter lies to hand. The duality between God and man becomes, as we have seen, in the light of God's Act, a triad. The whole meaning of the thought turns upon this triangular relation—God, man, and the Evil Reality. Now it is easy to say that what this really means (to our superior thought) is that God delivers man from the evil that is in his own heart, that is, from his own lower self. But this is merely to abolish one side of the triangle, and to break one of the remaining sides into two, in order to restore the triangle. It is a good example of explaining away, because the division of man into higher and lower, however true, is irrelevant to the present purpose. For *that* purpose man is a unit—though an internally discordant unit—and Sin is a factor over against him. Redemption is, fundamentally, redemption of the whole man. The thought of the higher and lower in man is relevant in the *description* of his disintegrated state (which calls for salvation) and of his several moral conflicts. But Christ saves the whole man, saves him from the disintegration of his wholeness.

In conclusion, let us note how, here again, the essentially ethical character of the Atonement appears, without the insertion of any synergistic modification to guard and to mar it. Forgiveness and personal renewal are brought under one formula, and each idea is enhanced in the enhancement of the other. The deliverance is God's *act* of forgiveness, and that from which we are delivered comprises *all* that comes between us and Him. The immediate, ultimate, and intermediate implications of this Forgiveness and Gift fall necessarily, as we hope our completed argument will show, into their right places.

CHAPTER XIV

THE CREDAL STRUCTURE

We have now to consider the general structure of the Christian creed, as it relates to the Person and Work of Christ: how it forms itself around the centre upon which we have taken up our position. We say *forms itself* with emphasis. For if—as it is our great object to show—the truths of Christianity are in fact one Truth, our chief intellectual task is an intensive scrutiny, before which barriers and scaffolding should melt away, and our ideal (however inadequately its attainment can be presented to others) to see each doctrine in the light of all. And, since an unfocused unity will always be imperfect, our understanding of the doctrine of the Cross claims to find its full attestation in its own *unique* relation to the other elements in the whole.

That the Cross—not as a general symbol but specifically and uniquely—takes this central place follows from the conclusions we have already reached. And here we have to note its relation to the Godhead. Even the vital truth that Christ *is* God is not so focal in the New Testament as that in Him God is the Saviour of the world. And nowhere is His Deity affirmed with more unqualified emphasis than in radically soteriological theology. The primary substance of Revelation is simply this transcendent Event, and the Godhead of Christ is its inevitable implication. The intimations of this, in the New Testament, are given as evidence of *some* transcendent fact concerning His status and relation to men: He interacts with them from a different plane. And, though the meaning of "Son of God" may be, from a later point of view, indefinite, the essential belief demanded is absolutely definite. The fact of His Coming was the fact of God's intervention. It is quite in accord with this that Socinianism, as is well known, began with a denial of the Atonement.

A Gospel is not, as such, a philosophy; and its implications, however vital, are not its cutting edge. But, after a little, the implications, when reflection turns upon them, come to be regarded more or less apart from one another. In this character they are expounded, defended and denied, and brought into relation with relevant, or seemingly relevant, ideas; and philosophical theologies arise, which, with all their defects, serve their purpose for a while, and then linger on like clinkers in a furnace. But may not the time have now arrived when we must ask whether the whole method has not become a clinker: whether we are not now called to an intensive search for the philosophy inherent in the Gospel, pivoted on its central meaning? Let us devote a few more words to the pivot before we go on to consider, from that view-point, the essential idea of the Incarnation.

<h1 style="text-align:center">I</h1>

From the standpoint of strictly theocentric theology, it is not difficult to see where the primary impact of the super-natural falls. We are accustomed to think and speak of the Incarnation and Resurrection as the great miracles, or wonders, of the Christian religion. But the one stupendous miracle is the Cross. For that is the essence of the thing that God did; and when we have said that God did it, we have by implication said all. There, in the consummated *Erniedrigung* of God—not in the intermediate stage, not in the return from Death—the real Divine paradox appears. But the idea of the Incarnation, in particular, demands some further study.

Passing over the humanitarian theologies, a little attention to what may be called the dominant orthodox idea of the Incarnation may enable us the more easily to define our own. The theology that belongs to it may reasonably claim to be, in its own way, a "Theology of the Incarnation", though for it the significance is very different from that indicated by Aulén. Let us start from the question: What is meant by the assumption of humanity by God? That we must posit such an act is unquestionable, if the Death of Christ has the meaning that we have seen in it. And, further, that meaning must give the clue to our answer.

The theory alluded to, which has long commended itself to many thinking minds in England, understands the Incarnation as essentially in itself the Divine Act of salvation, as directly significant of the greatness and possibilities of the race, as the pledge of the renewal of all life and of the sacredness of human relations. Considered in respect of its working, it is the provision of a regenerated humanity, secured and available in the Person of Christ. The interpretation of the Death of Christ is built up on this basis.

What then, if not this, it may be asked, is the "taking of the Manhood into God"? In answer, we must, as throughout, follow closely the line of "parsimony", not seeking a "rich" conception, but having regard to focus entirely, and neither lured nor deterred by the apparent philosophical implications of our terms. For, as we use them, they mean nothing but what is directly relevant to an *experience* of meaning which sublimates all the language that subserves it. But to proceed. The intensive *Fact* of the Divine descent to the depth of human nature and human need is the first call to our faith; and, if God reaches the deepest in man, He reaches the whole man. It is the doctrine of Creation, together with that of the Fall, that secures for us the scope and inclusiveness of the Christian Redemption. Man was created in the image of God: there was nothing good in man that God could take upon Himself, as if it were not in Him already. We believe, indeed, that the Incarnation restores to efficacy the creational purpose of God for man: something in it answers to what would anyhow have occurred. But we cannot possibly isolate this and argue from it. The Incarnation cannot be viewed apart from the Death, any more than the Death apart from the Incarnation.

The Redemptive Act was, most assuredly, carried out not

merely *for* man, but *upon* him. But we have dispensed with the idea of a substantive human race; and, even if we had not, it would not be adequate to our purpose. What Christ assumed, we are prepared to maintain, was, simply and literally, the single human Body. Does the New Testament —our inferences apart—tell us anything more than that? We hasten to add that this is not to be understood in any sort of Apollinarian sense. We may now be rid of the old idea that the body means the mere animal, or appetitive, part of our nature. We can regard it here as *one aspect of the whole*, barring freewill and all that it implies—a crucial question that we shall consider presently. We shall not get a coherent conception of the Incarnation unless we rigidly exclude redundancies. Christ could have assumed nothing that He had already, nor have given to man anything that man had already. What we seem to see that He really needed, and assumed, was human experience and the human medium of contact; that by which *ipso facto* His divine nature would become human also. Surely the human body answers the question as far as our minds are concerned: and this is all we want; for, if the answer is but relative to our human limitations, so is the question. The Body gave to Him individual membership of the race; and that this individual membership should, for Him, be also complete union, centrality, and headship is guaranteed from the side of His Deity. Starting from the fact that the body is the medium of social relations (which are of the essence of man), it ought not to be hard to realize that, *for Christ*, the appropriation of the one individual Body was the salvation of universal manhood.

This is how we meet the question asked, but not yet answered, in a previous chapter: How is it possible to reject the realistic conception of the race-as-a-whole and at the same time to regard the work of Christ as enacted upon the race, and not simply as the initiation of an agelong process from a point within it? The Birth was not the mystical assumption of a mystical entity: it was a kenosis. But, as matter is at once the limitation and the organ of spirit, so to Christ it was at once the self-negation by which He became one with a race whose very finitude, by reason of sin, divided it from its Creator, and also—Christ being what He is—the organ of a universal relationship to the actual concrete individualized humanity of all the ages. Thus, though the Body in which He passed through death was, as human, simply what each of our bodies is, yet in it He paved the way for mankind through life and death into the heavenly places. For it was a pledge and foretaste—just because *He* bore it—on behalf of all that visible creation of which, in itself, it was but an infinitesimal item.

It is regarded as almost a truism to say that Christ took upon Himself not merely a human body, but human nature. And, indeed, to affirm the bare assumption of the human body in any such sense as limits the range of the Incarnation has been rightly disallowed by the Church. The Apollinarian doctrine, which limited the act of Incarnation to the lower levels of human personality, is an instance of this defect. But it may be still asked whether the body, considered, not as a part or level, but as a side, or—with more direct relevance—as the point of contact, should not give us the direction of our thought. If we can find the point of attachment, the range can take care of itself.

And, if so, the nerve of the Divine paradox lies, not in what is taken, but in the taking of it. This runs counter to the view that the Divine Act is mediated by evolution. (And, even if evolution could produce in the end a perfect and ideal humanity, how could or can it give forth an individual so immensely in advance of the race in general as to be, in any intelligible sense, its Saviour? If we suppose such an "emergence" as that, we may as well discard the use of the idea of evolution altogether.) But it runs counter also, though within narrower limits, to such interpretation as sees in the object assumed any potential activity of universal manhood. In simple Redemptional Theology the Body is a unit among units, not in itself central or the organ of some very special product of the first creation: it is the focus, not of man's excellence, but of his need. What it became is what Christ made it, at once the first-fruits and the instrument of His Salvation, the seat of His Divine presence, and the nucleus of the redeemed humanity. Its assumption was indeed, in this sense, the assumption of the whole man, considered at once as individual and as the race. The Body, just because in itself negative and neutral, was the point of contact between the Redeemer and the total subject of His Redemption: with its evil, which He came to destroy, and its good, which He came, not to assist along an unbroken path from creation to maturity, but to deliver from the entanglement of sin and the inclusive ban of death.

But the humanity of Christ is considered to have another aspect in relation to our salvation: that is to say, the renewal and sustenance, directly, of our own humanity. Here, as before, we are obliged to reject the realistic conception. The precise idea that we dispute is that of the Divine-human life as descriptive of the Gift. It is a redundancy. What humanity requires is the divine, not the divine-human. Man is human already; and, though he has failed of the ideal of humanity, he does not need any new humanity, however glorified, but the regeneration in God of his own. God does not water the dry earth with wet earth, but with water. The duplication is meaningless. It is another form of the wrong understanding of the mediation of Christ's humanity between us and God. That mediation is to be seen in the entrance of the Redeemer into the race, as the ground and presupposition of His relations with the individual and the new Society. The humanity of Christ is the organ of the giving, not the substance of the Gift. (The idea which we are criticizing must not be confused with that of our incorporation into the humanity of Christ, which is absolutely true.)

How then shall we answer the oft-debated question

whether Christ became a Man or simply Man? The former alternative seems to conflict with the Deity of His Person, or to save it only by duplication; the latter to separate human nature from human personality, and to involve the paradox that He was human and personal, yet not a human person. The truth, we believe, is that the antithesis between the Divine and the human personality is unreal. He assumed human nature, at first neither personal nor universal, simply the unconscious infantile organism, with the human situation and experiences that it had in store for Him.

But, having reached this point, we now seem to see the Incarnation as not really completed by the assumption of the Body, and are ready to pass on to that aspect, already alluded to, in which its meaning is fulfilled.

It is part of human nature to be personal, individual, and therefore *free*. Incarnation must include the assumption of human freedom. But human freedom is not, like that of God, above crises and indeterminacy, and its victorious realization is not simply given with the body. It must win through, even in an organism possessed directly by God. Its victories there were real: they were neither necessities disguised as crises nor (of course) moral victories within the Godhead.

The old controversy between *posse non peccare* and *non posse peccare* need be no intrusion into things beyond our ken. However ignorant we may be, we must at least seek to know the frontiers of our ignorance, and its proper relation, at any given point, to the knowable. A mere vague agnosticism will not cut the Gordian knot of our difficulties. All that we have to do here is to try and show how our general conception of the Incarnation relates itself to this controversy, and just where, for us, the line runs between revealed and unrevealed mystery.

We have previously maintained that the absoluteness of God, as understood by a consistently theistic philosophy, yields the idea of perfect freedom without the necessity of supposing, after the event, that God might have acted otherwise. Now the triumph over temptation and the human acceptance of the Cross are surely the expression, within the Incarnate experience, of the Divine freedom. Here the *posse non*—therefore also the *posse*—holds, and it was not a delusion. Even the implied *posse* was real relatively to the human sphere. And this is no minimization of its reality. For, if it compels us to ask the question, "What if Christ had failed?" we might reply that such failure would not have belied the perfection of the Godhead, but have foreclosed its fulfilment in Jesus. But perhaps even that question lies, for us, beyond the mystery-line. Perhaps it is enough to say that the absolute freedom of the Divine will must, in the human and temporal sphere, take the form of indeterminacy, which corresponds, in human volition, to the absoluteness of the Divine; and that God took to Himself the experience of choice. The moral victories of Christ, then, were not the process of fashioning a representative human perfection, but phases of the supreme Divine conflict for our emancipation, which reached its crisis at the Cross and its victory at the Resurrection.

Thus it may be said that these moral victories are common elements alike of the Incarnation and of the Atonement. Without them both the one and the other would be incomplete and ultimately unintelligible.

II

And, as with the Incarnation before the Cross, so with the Resurrection after it. The Easter festival, as Aulén has truly remarked, is the stronghold of the classic view of the Atonement. For the Cross, which was by its own meaning a victory, would not have been so without the Resurrection, or even thinkable as the act of God. And the Resurrection without the Atonement sinks into mere dogma or mere mythology, or to the symbolism of a theology that would never have used such if it had not had it on its hands. The Divine paradox, the clear-cut factuality, that made it a *Gospel* to the first disciples, is given back to us only *within* the total paradox of Redemption, of which the centre is the Cross.

The Ascension is equally inevitable. This is not another doctrine than that of the Resurrection: they are one fact, containing a temporal interim, more mysterious than either. The belief in this fact is only the other side of the belief in the Incarnation. These elements in the Creed together bring the Sacrifice and the Triumph into direct relation to human history and human needs, and form the link between the implicit Victory of the past and the explicit Victory of the future. In short, the solidarity of these items of belief does not require to be reached—and cannot properly be reached— by merely fitting them together, but only by the analysis of the simple idea of Redemption, accepted, with all its implications, as one intelligible Truth.[1]

III

But our basis remains incomplete till we have given some consideration to the doctrine of the Holy Spirit, and tried to show how this—and therefore the Trinitarian conception— is essential to Theism, at the last analysis.

We have had something to say, at previous stages, about the idea of Immanence, in two aspects: in relation to nature and in relation to moral goodness. And, at least in the latter case, we have not been able to accept this physical analogy as a desirable instrument of our thought. But here, it may be said, we really do require something of the kind. Transcendentalism seems to leave a residuum which is all the more insistent in its claims because it has been so definitely pressed

---

[1] The narratives of the visible occurrences associated with the several phases of the Redemptive Act, in their relation to faith and its doctrinal content, need hardly come into our discussion. The meanings that they *have in fact* conveyed are the essential thing.

back to its own frontier. And is not the Holy Spirit essentially *God in us*?

This is true, but, even so, we are not dependent upon the word, and it may be well to avoid it instead of all the time dodging its pitfalls. And somehow it does not seem natural to most of us to apply the idea of immanence in this connection, even though we readily use the word "in". For indeed the presence of the Holy Spirit is rather—if we may use the expression—transcendent *a tergo* than immanent. Or, it is so utterly deep as to be not so much within as beneath. But, to understand the doctrine of the Holy Spirit, the essential thing, in our opinion, is to face the question that is so often shunned, namely its distinction from that of the risen and self-revealing Christ.

The Word, the Gospel, the Divine Saviour, *confront* us. Christ is the direct object of trust and love. He is the Light of the world. The Church, we are told, is the "Spirit-bearing Body", and *in* the Church the individual partakes of His light and life. We do not, however, admit the common antithesis between the individual and the social. We understand the presence of the Spirit as in the direct sense a presence to the individual, but at the same time a presence *by virtue of which he is a member of the one Body*, and therefore a true individual and not an atom.

The Church has no Ego of its own (otherwise it could not be the Body of *Christ*); therefore we cannot use the idea of the "mind of the Church" without caution. And certainly it is an external object to the mind of the reflective individual, and cannot supersede or effect the opening of his own eyes. This even the glorified Christ, whose Body the Church is, cannot do, except as the Sender of the Spirit. For—to put it in simple language—Christ is in Heaven, we and the Spirit on earth.

In brief, *Christ is God on the Church's side of its Godward relation: the Holy Spirit is God on the individual's side of his Christward relation.*

IV

We thus reach the Trinitarian doctrine. We approach it from two sides. First on the side of the tripersonal relation to ourselves. We have seen that the Divine personality—or selfhood—is apprehended over against, and in relation to, our own. We note this in three different ways, which relate respectively to the three Persons: to the Father as the object, normally, of our personal communion (the "I—Thou relation"); to the Son through the medium of the Incarnation; to the Holy Spirit as our own Alter Ego. There is no need, or justification, for introducing abstract or metaphysical theories that go beyond the requirements of this directly redemptional theology. For the eternal side of the Divine personality, in each of its aspects severally, is secured by the implications of that theology.

Sabellianism has the attractions of a simple doctrine that seems to preserve untouched the full divinity of Christ without incurring any charge of Tritheism. But, at the first moment when we turn reflection upon the credal experience of the Nicene Christian (its logic, not its genesis), we see that the threefold idea supports it like three pillars upon no one or two of which alone it could rest. What we mean is exactly expressed in words of St Paul which give the Trinitarian faith in a nutshell: "Through Him we both have our access in one Spirit unto the Father" (Eph. ii. 18). In fact, what we have said about the Divine Person of the Son—and so of each Person severally—applies to the eternal distinction between the Persons. It is final *for us*, and therefore, if indeed Revelation is the final word, is really final. For even to affirm alternative possibilities, so far from being a humble confession of our ignorance, would be an unwarranted claim for human thought.

If therefore the distinctness as here conceived presents to some a certain anthropocentric appearance, we can plead that this anthropocentricity is only the refusal to "tread the vacuum of mid-air" (if we may adopt the conjectural emendation of the text of Col. ii. 18), instead of standing to view the Revelation at the angle at which it was given. And those who believe that Revelation is above all the Revelation of the *redeeming* God, and that the ultimate truth of His very Being is in the long run pivoted upon the Cross, will see in His redemptive relation to men the very meaning of what He is. They will know nothing of any gap between His acts and His essence.

Certainly, if the triunity is essential to the Godhead, and yet the idea of it reaches us only by way of God's relation to us His creatures, we are committed to the positive answer to the old question: "Is it essential to God that He should create?" For the created *mind* has thus an essential place. The very last word about the very Being of God is that given by Revelation *to us* and in terms of an Act wrought for and upon us. And God cannot be thought of as doing anything incidentally. We know nothing of a non-creative God, any more than of a non-atoning God, even by way of hypothesis.

This is the one angle of approach, and in its foreground is the *distinction* of the Divine Persons. But it must be completed by some positive answer to the question of the unity, which is the correlative idea, and a matter of intellectual experience caused and directed by the contact of Revelation.

In the chapter on *The Content of the Idea of God* we touched upon the subject of superpersonality. Our main object then was to reject any conception of it which relegated personality to the limbo of half-truths, which we do not so much hold as find ourselves unable to avoid. We indicated, however, a positive aspect of superpersonality—its inclusion of forms of the Good which, while themselves sub-personal, are not clearly gathered up into personality. Here we must be prepared to see personality surrender its *own* unity—the single person—and submit itself to a higher unity in which it is adjectival only.

It is sometimes said that, while it is right to speak of God as personal, it is not right to speak of Him as a Person. We believe that this distinction is absolutely correct, and a useful indication of the true direction of our thought in the matter. It implies, as we adopt it, that neither is God *three* Persons, regarded as externally interrelated, as we are. Trinitarianism is satisfied by two simple affirmations on this point: that the distinctions are objective and eternal; and that they do not divide the Personality into portions of personality.

If we adhere to the doctrine of the Divine Persons as generally accepted in the Church, and at the same time to the unity of the Godhead, we *must* think of God as super-personal. Nothing but what is beyond even concrete personality—the infinite Concrete—can hold together in our minds the tripersonality. It still remains that—as we have said before—personality is the roof of the house we are in, open to the sky. Along the line that we apprehend it there is nothing beyond. But it is known to us essentially in worship, that is—as Heim and others have driven home to us—in an "I—Thou" relationship, not primarily in the (grammatical) third person. And worship is not the whole relation we bear to God, and cannot stand by itself. We speak and think *of* God, even when we affirm that He is "Thou". And, since this predicative relation occupies part of the ultimate ground that we stand on, and the other would break up altogether without it, we must take full account of it. So far, indeed, as concerns this treatise, the theocentric position, behind yet involving the Trinitarian distinctions, is maintained, consistently we hope, throughout.

We claim for this view, of course, that it is not merely theoretical, but can be, and is, realized in Christian experience. The God we think *about*—when we are not thinking of one of the Persons in the proper context of the thought—is surely personal but not a particular Person. If we try to think of God as a Person abstractly, our imagination is apt to palm off upon us a mean and irreverent anthropomorphism. And yet, on the other hand, the tripersonality also is not an abstractly external fact, understood on the basis either of some tripartite analysis of human nature or of human interpersonal relations. It means, so far as we can see, simply this: that, just as, in the finite personality, the Ego-centre is the fixed point of reference, transcending all in man that is composite and interactive, so, in the infinite Personality, even this centre itself is transcended. To endeavour to retain its inclusiveness and centrality here, as on the human level, is to obscure and restrict the self-revelation of the Name that is above every name.

Persons may be—and they are—the highest known forms of finite reality, but God Himself is above all forms in His creation. When we say "God", we utter the one final term of Being, the prius and the key to all those terms with which our philosophy seeks to build up its idea *about* God. To say that God is personal yet not a Person or society involves no contradiction. It is simply an arrest of thought—such an arrest as we meet when the Divine supersedes the human, when the half-dug vineyard discloses the treasure, when, athwart our programmes, in the second watch or in the third watch, the Lord shall come. As human virtue does not shade off into holiness, as human progress does not discover Heaven, so human thought does not think out Revelation. A superfluous word is a false word. "God is in Heaven and thou on earth: therefore let thy words be few."

CHAPTER XV

THE ESCHATOLOGICAL STANDPOINT

The revival of evangelic theology is the revival of Eschatology. The issue involves, directly or indirectly, the whole economy of grace, not future only. And at the same time it requires that the real future must never be explained away. The "eternal future" of Barth's earlier phase, that seems above rather than at the end of Time, is, if strictly taken, no true future at all. Barth's emphasis on this (for it may be no more than emphasis) is now replaced or supplemented by a more direct eschatological reference. At any rate, we are here concerned to claim for Eschatology both a true reference to what *will* be—the second and final phase of the one Redemptive Act—and therewith a better view-point for the understanding of the past phase and also of the Divine activity that moves along the time-gap between.

We cannot, of course, envisage completely any change that concerns the temporal sphere as such, in advance of its occurrence. There is no detached standpoint from which we can view it; for "*we* shall be changed", mentally no less than physically. The whole subject, however, is intensely interesting, especially now that our thinking is equipped with the conception of multi-dimensional time. But we cannot here enter into the subtleties of this subject, and choose therefore a different mode of approach.

The future is apprehended in *expectation*, and expectation is a definite form of experience. Without it futurity would be meaningless, no less than *vice versâ*. (This is, of course, none the less true though we may say of a man that certain things, unexpected by himself, *were* in store for him in the future.) Shall we then, instead of constructing or accepting a prophetic programme claiming a purely objective rationality, try to understand the meaning and significance of expectation, or hope, as a primary element of Christian faith and experience?

We use the word "hope" in the New Testament sense; that is, without any implication of uncertainty. What we have said in the first chapter about faith in this connection applies equally to hope: it is inherently absolute and unqualified, however imperfect and unstable our own exercise and experience of it may be. Faith lays hold of supertemporal reality in which a temporal future is directly implicated.

As to the general objection—applied to the Incarnation especially—that the idea of an entrance of Eternity into Time is self-contradictory, it leaves us untouched. We refuse to treat the concrete terms of religion as if they were the abstract antitheses of philosophy. Eternity and Time, as mere philosophical ideas, are, it is true, shaped by contradistinction to one another, and cannot interfuse. But Eternity, for theology, means God and His Kingdom in relation to world-conditions. And, if once we accept the double idea of the creation of the world—that is, of the Time-sphere—by eternal Being and of its entrance into that sphere, need we stumble at that of its future entrance to re-create? But we shall deal further with this side of the subject later in the chapter.

I

But before we proceed to consider the intrinsic significance of the eschatological outlook, a few words must be said about its position in the New Testament. That the primitive form of the Christian Gospel was structurally, not incidentally, eschatological, seems sufficiently clear. No doubt there are the three original lines of anticipation, which we ought not to confuse: the Growth of the Kingdom, the End of the World, and the Coming of the Son of Man. And we may admit that any unification of these *would* be confusion if it found short cuts from one idea to the other, instead of following each of them to its estuary. But whether there be or be not one estuary—whether their confluence is incidental or is essential to an inclusive Divine meaning—is another question.

Again, the significance of this primitive stratum is obscured by the peculiar rationalistic approach to the New Testament to which we are habituated. That there is a certain philosophical development in—for instance—St Paul's thought cannot be denied, nor that he becomes less naïvely eschatological. God's truth needed to strike its roots deeper into the soil of the human mind. But this fact must be balanced by another. The new does not wholly refine or absorb the old. In a sense, Divine truth is less compromised by naïve symbolism than by the refinements of the higher thought. God has hid from the wise and prudent what He has revealed unto babes. The symbol is mere sensuous expression. It is passive. The thinking has its own rights, and, even at its best, ever tends to turn the message into a theory. The one lies closer to the primary immediacy, the other becomes entangled in the liabilities, and is lured by the ideals, of human reflection. But all thought in the New Testament is anchored to fact; and, even if the factual structure does historically—whether we like it or not—include a catastrophically depicted future, surely the structure claims our understanding as a whole, before its parts come into question.

It is easy to dismiss Eschatology—especially under the name "apocalyptic"—as a mere carnival of trumpets and fireworks, as a brass band that plays outside our study window and disturbs our reflection, and to pass on to the congenial and refined spirituality of the Fourth Gospel and the later Pauline Epistles. But those who do fail to note that the very externality, crudity, and materiality which are the cover for the rejection of the whole point of view are the witness to their own inconsequence, and therefore to the superficiality of mere rejection, or substitution of generalities. We shall find it a worthier, not a less worthy, task for our intellectual discernment and analysis to penetrate objectively into the essential "intention" of the whole than to treat it as a mere adaptation of our deeper and more lofty creed to obsolete forms of Jewish thought. Just *because* God's Truth is above Time, it can speak for all time in the language of a passing hour.

Not, of course, that it is wrong to regard e.g. the Fourth Gospel as the high-water mark of an infinitely valuable advance in the New Testament itself. But this is human appraisement of human achievement, however divinely enlightened both the one and the other may be. Advance is *in* Time. And surely the more divine the things that our progressive thought has to handle, the harder it is for it —yet the more necessary—to take up the new without letting go some of the old. If the Fourth Gospel is related to the rest of the New Testament simply as the last of a spiritual series, that series must be regarded either as arbitrarily terminated or as on the plane of post-canonical reflection throughout the ages, whatever the gap between. In either case, the idea of an articulate "Word of God" is lost. It may indeed seem that the doctrine of the "Last Things" (especially if John v. 28 and 29 is an interpolation) has in that book entered upon the highest stage of a process of sublimation. But is there no structural residuum, and, if so, what? If faith, as we are trying to show, really grasps directly an intuited whole of truth, it must look *first* to the integrity and coherence of the outline of the vision, and then to spiritual clarification and deepening. Now the Fourth Gospel, with all its philosophical and mystical insight, is nothing if not centred upon visible and factual reality. We do not deny that the cruder passage must be revised in the light of the more spiritual, but the influence must be mutual. That the believer "shall not come into the judgement" implies the judgement, and the more we emphasize its radicality and finality, the greater the significance of the exemption. To slur the idea of a "Last Judgement" is to slur the idea of all judgement, and to slur that is to slur the idea of grace.

Judgement is by the very idea of it two-sided: and whether we say that the believer is raised above it or that he is acquitted and rewarded depends upon the plane of thought on which we are thinking. That the former plane is the higher we do not hesitate to say, but the fullness of its meaning depends upon our adequate conception of the Judgement into which the believer "shall not come". If we stumble at the paradox of its reality as at once factual and unimaginable, let us not say too much till, in our experience, the paradox of its factual *remission* has released for us the new vision of God.

It may not be wrong to say that supernatural events—those foretold and those recorded—are symbolic expressions of super-temporal truths. But the term symbol is inadequate and may easily mislead. It suggests parallel rather than contact. We certainly do not desire to anchor our faith, after the old manner, to a sporadic supernaturalism which tends to make the Incarnation a miracle, however supreme, among miracles. As against this, but also as against the tendency to parallelize, we understand the relation intensively—as punctual contact. The supernatural penetrates, does not spread, except as the ripples spread when a stone is thrown into the water. But, just because Redemption is *one Fact*, we must be sure that we do not mutilate the meaning of the one Fact. For there is no gap in its *meaning*, though, being in Time, it is also penetrated and divided by time. And it is the plea of this chapter that the Divine future is a structural reality of the Gospel, on equal terms with the present and the past. Indeed, in the New Testament, the future phase is itself "the Redemption".

The Johannine teaching is a re-interpretation, not of the promise of the Return, but of its nearness. "He shall show you things to come." True, indeed, the Divine Spirit places the human in a position of detachment relatively to the forms in which the primary Gospel was given. But this detachment means two things: not only the (true) intellectual freedom, but a clear synoptic view of the (to us) original Gospel as an object *over against us*. It does not therefore mean a licence to rationalize. The naïver forms of thought—the more discontinuous with our own—are better witnesses to an object external to us and to them than those which meet us on our own plane. For indeed the Other Paraclete transcends our minds no less than He who sent Him. And that very detachment, wherein the message of God is accepted as one articulate truth, demands the integrity of that truth before even the most spiritual re-statement of it begins.

Of course, to say this is not to demonstrate directly the inclusion of a definite Eschatology in the main structure of Christian belief. But we may say with confidence that, for those who do accept as pivotal the idea of a Divine redemptive intervention, known in the nature of the case only by a Revelation which is a part of it, there can be but one answer to the question. The doctrine of the Return is no mere corollary, or something which can be explained *into* some other element in the total idea: rather, its denial or subordination is a gaping breach in the walls. It is not by chance that a simple belief in the direct saving action of God in the past and in the present tends in actual experience to co-exist with the Advent hope. These interact upon one another, because they have a common basis. It is a cheap achievement to discredit them when divided.

Dr Barry says of the Apocalyptists: "However we may wish to disagree either with their methods or with their conclusions, at least they have given us a Prince and a Saviour (Acts v. 31), girt about with majesty and awe." But the ideas that a theology "gives" it gives in its own context and on its own terms.

This, then, is the *primâ facie* challenge of Eschatology. What its actual significance is remains a task for reflection, a task rendered harder at first, not easier, by the fact that the subject lies so close to our eyes in the primary givenness of Revelation. But we have prejudiced already the issue of the enquiry if we lapse into the method of subjective valuation determined by an evolutionistic and monistic theo-cosmology. For the message, whatever it is, *confronts* our finite minds, at their highest and at their lowest alike.

We have now to consider two things: first, the direct significance of the eschatological view; then the conception of history and grace which we reach by way of it.

II

Our central proposition relating to the former of these two enquiries is this: the ultimate Future is the *actuality* of Redemption in its wholeness, and thus the incorporation of the very conditions and framework of spiritual experience and of our bodily, spatial, and social life. No reality can be fully concrete that does not gather this up. For even our most transcendent mystical experiences and our truest and deepest ideas are, on one side of them, temporal facts that occur within that sphere. The absolute future is not the prolongation of the past, but its transformation. And this includes its material basis, by which all else is conditioned. It is the Resurrection of the whole.

Our religious thoughts, apart from hope, live half amid the fragments and half in the mist. "All things", says St Paul, "*are* yours"—now; but, as we have seen in a previous chapter, the Now never realizes its true meaning: it is always either a span, *containing* a before and after, or an elusive indivisible point. Though we have maintained that God is apprehended in the true present, yet there remains the strange truth that the real present is not itself present to be captured and retained. It cannot make good its own meaning within the time-stream, and, in this very breakdown, gives us a side-glimpse of eternity. But the future has no such kink. True, it *is* not present; but then, by its very meaning, it does not pretend to be. It is an anchorage of thought in a way that the present can never be. God, of course, is above this anomaly: but we are not God, and never shall be.

It would be difficult, perhaps, to exaggerate the sustaining and vitalizing power which genuine Christian hope exercised upon many minds in the days when the idea of a "Word of God" was clear-cut. This mysticism of hope, as we may call it, has as great a claim to respect as the mysticism of present immediacy. And it has this advantage: that the failure to establish itself, which keeps mystic experience, in spite of itself, an incident in temporal life, and which tantalizes spiritual aspiration, is in hope focused, accepted, and overcome.

Only to faith as hope is the content of the promise in Christ presented in terms of completeness and victorious possession. In all else, it will always be eked out, sampled, mediated, symbolized. And indeed it is only because our foretastes are foretastes, and give themselves to us as such, that their substance is not compromised by the imperfection of their form. Who can measure the loss to our sense of the reality, and therefore of the presence, of Christ that we unconsciously sustain by our loose hold on the promise of His Return?

The unrealized Christ, "whom having not seen we love", the Christ veiled only by our want of faith—infinitely mighty, none the less, and infinitely near—seems more to us than the future Christ. But the very veil that hides Him, the dullness, deadness, and unbelief that exclude Him—all this is part of the very darkness and death that He came to destroy. It is right that we should contrast His objective nearness and saving power with our subjective deadness to Him. But *a subjective state is an objective fact*. And this fact belongs to the very situation which the Redemptive Act confronts. Only in overcoming the state will the Act reach full actuality.

All who are familiar with Otto's *Idea of the Holy* will remember how the "mysterium tremendum" is one of the elements into which the experience of the Holy falls when we analyse that in it which is accessible to our analysis. There is an extraordinary connection between awe and intimacy in the experience of God. All the connecting links which our reason or our symbolic imagination supplies to us are, after all, separative also. Thus it is that even the most extravagant assertions of God's unknowableness sometimes serve to show Him to us as so far off that the infinite distance itself saves us by self-despair, and we see Him as *absolutely* near just because He has bridged an *infinite* gulf. Such mysticism may be Christian or not very distinctively Christian. But at least it sets a problem that the Gospel answers. God has actually bridged the gulf—as we learn by faith, which is beyond all mysticism—with a bridge of three arches: the Incarnation with the Cross, the Ascension, and the Return. In this revelation the mystery and the light, the distance and the nearness, the transcendence and the intimacy, the awfulness and the love, close into one. Of these three phases the third— the Return or "Appearing"—makes the two former explicit, and the anticipation of it is essential to their meaning. Without it the progressive inward revelation of Christ—even the glorified Christ—expanding through the ages of the future life, could afford no substitute. We cannot progress to the absolute. In the end it must absorb and supersede any auxiliary divine light within us. Man will then know God by nature, for his nature will be perfected. And if indeed the majesty and glory of God are revealed, as we believe, in terms of humanity, such revelation is still abstract and remote, untrue to its own purport, if that humanity itself is never to be revealed in its *absolute* Divine meaning.

Why then the prevailing difficulty about the "personal" Coming? Either Christ will come or He will not. And to suppose an impersonal coming would be a descent to a lower plane of religious belief. Why is it harder to believe in a second manifestation of God than in the first? It may transcend personality, but by so much the more will it contain it.

Eschatologism re-acts against the modern pre-occupation with the divine *within* the human. Its interest is in the *exit in infinitum* in Christ and of Christ, the exit that leaves us waiting for His Return. This is not mere theory or intellectual predilection. It is the final logic of a Christianity that means centrally the Redemptive Act of God. God is known to us in Christ, not in the sense of Spiritual Evolutionism, but just because, having descended, He has ascended, and a cloud has received Him out of our sight.

III

We can now proceed to consider the re-action of the eschatological idea upon our general view of grace and providence. The first thing to be said is that all language that we use—and sometimes are obliged to use—respecting God's action which makes it appear subsidiary, indirect, or even progressive, is relative to our own point of view and to the particular occasions of our need. God's action, *as such*, falls upon—does not work within—the time-order. Conditioned it certainly is; and this, rightly understood, gives us all that the facts require. In dealing with the subject of Evil, we applied to it directly the truth that God is the Author of all reality *so far as* it is good; and this qualification implies that the activity of God is, in the time-sphere, conditioned, therefore deflected and delayed. A consistently God-to-man theology comes to this, we are sure, in the end. Even progress is not as such good: it makes for the relatively good, which in itself may in the long run only enhance the resources of evil. Fundamentally, it is the delay of the End: the End is not the outcome of progress. It is not enough to begin by explaining the Coming of Christ as a series of superimposed crises and revivals, and then to place the unique Event at the top as a fitting crown or coping-stone. It is the latter that is the πρῶτον ἡμῖν, the fact directly related to the Resurrection and Ascension. All between is as the wire to the posts.

No doubt one strand in the New Testament Eschatology is the thought in the Synoptic Gospels of the Kingdom as growing. But two questions, closely connected, need to be asked. First, does the Kingdom as such emerge, or develop

,

out of human life and history; and not rather, all through, *come* from above? Secondly, is not the growth a growth rather to a "harvest" of the elect: to a separation of wheat and tares: to a harvest *and* a vintage, than that of a divine world-order? Surely, our Lord's teaching, even on this special side, by no means suggests a development of the higher elements of the world-life, or a goal continuous with those elements. The kingdom is not *of* this world, even of the best within it. In short, our answer to this second question brings to light two complementary ideas. There is the growth of the new community, or new religion—or however we may put it—confronting a rival kingdom, openly or covertly hostile, which may wax stronger rather than weaker in face of the counter-growth; and this none the less though evil is mixed with the good and good with the evil. And then there is the Event which decides the issue—the Judgement, the Harvest, the inauguration-feast of Eternity. We cannot fuse these two conceptions: they are correlated as before and after. But they cast their light towards each other over the dark waste between.

Both are necessary, not only to the whole idea but to each other. The Advent is essentially a Judgement, the separation of the wheat from the tares, the final Divine analysis, which shall extricate and establish the true and ultimate values of the Kingdom of Heaven. In its primary Advent the Kingdom appealed to the human will. The Second Advent is never conceived as including an appeal to the will: it lies on the further side of the will. The progress of the Kingdom on earth requires the second explicit Act of God, as truly as it requires the former Act. We have already controverted the idea of the self-salvation of the race or the individual, even though "enabled" by the precedent or concomitant action of God. This Act of God, regarded in its fullness and as fully His, must sooner or later become explicit. The immanent and hidden character of the Kingdom on earth is not ultimate. It is temporal, and therefore temporary.

To accept Time simply as a bracketed interval, necessary as such, but containing its own conditions which may be ended even when incompletely fulfilled, seems all that is necessary for our purpose. Probably we cannot understand the principle that decides the maturity of the Harvest. The secret of that day and that hour belongs to the hidden wisdom of God, whether we think of that secret as hidden in the highest heaven, or in the deepest depths of creation and of man.

Indeed, if we do not understand the growth of the Kingdom somewhat thus, there seems to be no reconciling it with any of those ideas that centre round the Coming of the Son of Man. And it is the latter—released from all bondage to physical imagery—that most obviously squares with the root-idea of intervention, which is now at last refusing to be kept in the back place to which it has so long been relegated by traditional Modernism. For, as we have already pleaded, the two assents of faith, directed to the two Acts of Redemption (or Comings of Christ) respectively, sustain one another, for the simple reason that the two Acts are one Act; and so, when the dirempted whole is seen in its integrated unity—the dividing time as bracketed in eternity—the two assents become one assent.

Thus it is that the future casts a divine light before it upon the events of history and personal life. The Kingdom itself does not evolve (even its growth is a coming), but it necessarily exhibits the essential characteristics of that world-life in which it materializes. Spiritual life and spiritual corporate activity cannot be thought of as real unless as also tending to progress. Foretastes are necessary where there is indefinite delay. But the Kingdom transcends even the purest currents—purified by itself—of the world-life. It remains, relatively even to these, intervention.

Let us try to see just *how* the direct eschatological reference affects our view of the things that lie between. It does so by the light that it throws upon the meaning of faith. For we see now: first, that hope is an essential element in faith; secondly, that hope (of course in its specifically Christian sense) must have as its immediate and primary object the explicit and final Act of God.

Hope is essential to faith. Faith, it is true, has ever to tell itself that God is near though we are blind to Him: that Christ is knocking at a door that *we* do not open to Him: that, in the words of a Persian mystic, our "Where art Thou?" is God's "Here I am". But this is only one side of the matter. An attitude of deliberate, vigilant waiting—not hanging on *in spite of* delay—is one side of faith itself. There are things, such as forgiveness, that we immediately *take*. There are things for which we must wait. There are things that sometimes wait for our taking and sometimes are ours only for the waiting. All this belongs to the logic and fact of Christian experience. Here we are simply concerned with the broad truth that, as a matter of fact, less than the whole Gift is present for our taking: that faith, itself and as such, is a waiting as well as a taking. For, though it may be said, from one point of view, that nothing stands between us and full triumph but the limitation of our faith, yet this limitation is surely rooted in the very conditions that call for faith. For faith embraces the Whole, yet not in its wholeness. Even apart from our personal sinfulness, God is not revealed in His fullness. The implication of the individual in a social life and environment, the social character of the revelation which is delivered to him, all this is one aspect of this limitation. And surely it should be a great relief to those who are wearied with the apparent elusiveness of the things that claim to be the nearest and freest, with the seeming silence of a God who is always more ready to hear than we to pray, to realize that expectation, or waiting, is not a secondary form of faith, but of its essence. Faith would be stultified, and belie itself, without hope.

But, it may be said, the direct and essential object of faith is God Himself. Simple self-committal does not look for promises and assurances outside the Giver. Just as it finds present joy in God without grasping for joy *by means of* God, so also the joy of the future needs not to be brought into the focus, but can be left to take care of itself. To some minds even immortality can be allowed to remain in the shadows, so long as we maintain a bare trust attitude without any content but God Himself, and keep alive our desire for His communion and service. Have we not, after all, tended to substitute the experience of God, as an object of faith, for God Himself?

But this objection really condemns all trust in God for anything that is nameable apart from Himself. Most assuredly the great things that we trust and hope for *are* not apart from, but in, God. But they *are* in Him. To say that we must seek Him for what He is in Himself does not disallow the question —however partial the answer may be—*what* God is in Himself. The Psalmist answered it, in the name of countless others, when he said: "In Thy presence is the fullness of joy." To say that all spiritual joys are in God is not to say that they may be ignored as if they were outside Him. And so with hope. For what God *will* give, and the fact that He will give it, are as truly of His essence as the things that He does give.

And His giving is self-giving; that is, finally, His coming. To wait for that is to wait for the experience of it, and *vice versâ*. To distinguish the two would be meaningless. If we carried through the abstraction of the idea of God from that of the experience of Him, we should have to deny that even communion with Him itself should be a conscious ideal. And not to seek that is not to seek Him.

Much of the content of faith is, it is true, relative, and, in a peculiar sense, uncertain. There are things—about the future life especially—which are to us a matter of faith; really so, even though reason may have had a share in clearing our way to them. They have a real solidarity with the central certainties. But they are as things seen in a mist. As expressible ideas, or rational formulations, we are rightly diffident about them, even though, at the bottom of our minds, we know that a golden thread connects them somehow with the heart of reality. But this marginal faith presupposes focal faith. And hope itself is focal, not marginal; for its object is the Eternal, that transcends, but does not abolish, Time. Without it, faith must ever tend to feed upon the experiences it has won: to cling to after-images: to dilute itself with opinion.

IV

We are now in a position to add something to what we have said earlier in the chapter, concerning the relation of Eternity to Time. Non-eschatological theology continually tends, in spite of itself, to treat Eternity in terms of prolonged time. Having firmly put down the crude idea of "mere everlastingness", it relegates eternity to bare supertemporality, the next crudest idea. Thought that is dominated by the conceptions of growth and attainment cannot readily contemplate a vertical descent of the Eternal upon our uncompleted processes. Thus comes in the process *in* Eternity, or, to put it the other way, an eternal ascent in Time. For the delays, sub-processes, inhibitions—all the conditions and stages of our inner life while on earth—present themselves as a programme necessary somehow to be worked *through* before the goal is reached. This is only one way in which the close connection between a crypto-Semi-Pelagianism and the attenuation of Eschatology can be traced.

And even then the goal does not easily appear as final, if our thoughts are controlled by the idea of immanent process. The dimensional principle, however inadequate in direct relation to ultimate Truth, does at least release us from these ruts. When it is said "I could not endure an eternity without progress, purpose, and continual gains", or even "I could not endure everlasting existence at all", the real question has been missed. By hypothesis the New Order would not include boredom or dissatisfaction. It would be the fullness of life. The question is whether this consummation itself can be made the object of genuine and grounded expectation. And it is just this question that we refuse to consider in isolation from the total meaning of the Christian Redemption and from the truth-claim of the faith that answers to it.

Still, having introduced the ideas of Time and Eternity, one over against the other, we recognize the need for philosophical clarity. We have already denied that the entrance of Eternity into Time—or rather of the eternal world into the time-world—is just the transition, factually conceived, of one member of a metaphysical antithesis to another. Since, however, the two terms *are* applicable severally to the two interacting spheres, we must add something more, on the lines of Heim. Eternity, as the religious mind knows full well, is already in Time. That which is implicit in life and history—a mere factor, or subterraneous force upheaving—will come to its own and be supreme. And that must be balanced by the converse: namely, that the Time-principle will then be within, and subordinated to, the eternal. The upper will be under and the under upper. The temporal things that are necessary to our complete life will be gathered up. So even progress itself, if it is one of these, has something in it, elusive to *our* analysis, that will be incorporated in the Perfect that will come. This is quite a different view from that which substitutes for the End a series of ends punctuating a line of advance that itself has no end. And note that it does not in the least compromise the true eschatological antithesis on which we have insisted. For this antithesis does not imply that there is no eternal element in Time, any more than that there is no good in our fallen world. It is the total *relation* between Time and Eternity that will be reversed.

But the End cannot be conceived by any metaphysical construction. Still less historically or astronomically. It transcends the world of thought and nature alike. But it is not therefore alien and irrelevant. Just because it is so revolutionary, it is conservative. We need look for no sensational crash in history, no collision of heavenly bodies, no violent rupture of the internal continuities of experience; for it transcends the plane on which these things happen, and the minds that encounter or expect them.

And, if it transcends catastrophe, assuredly it transcends even spiritual progress and effort. These things, and all that goes with them, are necessary in the time-sphere, but Time does not wait for them. Sin is deeper than those temperamental, quasi-physical disabilities, inherited or incurred, which effort and discipline can overcome. That is the true ground both of our pessimism and of our optimism. That is why it eludes and baffles us, and ever re-enters by hidden doors when it has been expelled. But that also makes intelligible a Divine Death that has undermined it and an Advent before which it will collapse.

To conclude with a retrospective glance at our main thesis. The essence of the Advent faith is not the retention of unassimilable elements with which a moral or mystical Christianity can dispense. It is the simple refusal to break up the one unitary idea of Redemption. We have tried throughout to commend an intensive and organic interpretation of the Christian creed, no longer disintegrated by eschatological theories which reduce the future phase to terms of continuity with the present, or find in it only the dramatic expression of a principle. For, even though this be the very counter-principle to a one-sided doctrine of development: though it be that of real conflict of Good against Evil —sporadic in Time, absolute above Time—the essential idea is not satisfied. If faith is not anchored to the real Concrete, the Future that is not made but *comes*, if its field is distributed in Time or suspended in an unchanging Eternity, we are still drifting with a stream that can flow anywhere—except uphill.

Meanwhile the key to that Future is the indwelling Spirit of Him who raised up Jesus from the dead. We know only

in part, but we know that we know in part: the parts confess
themselves as such and promise the whole. But we can never
reach the Whole. Progress belongs to the sphere of the partial,
and cannot lead out of that sphere. When that which is
perfect is *come*, then that which is in part shall be done
away.

CHAPTER XVI

RETROSPECT AND CONCLUSION

The aim of this book has been to understand the Christian faith as a focused unity: to commend this presentment, not by coercive demonstration, but by releasing an intellectual intuition that, in its turn, once truly realized, must take control of the rational processes that assisted its emergence. It is our conviction that the whole content of the Christian meaning of Redemption is one inclusive and indiscerptible whole—that Redemption and Revelation may, from the side of either, be brought under one formula—however little we may have succeeded in bringing this home even to sympathetic readers. Further, we are sure (though this could not be worked out in a small space) that this conception gives unity to our general philosophy of life, reality, and knowledge, by breaking up illicit or provisional unities that Philosophy has formed within itself, and opening out *from the other side* its convergent blind alleys.

God's Truth, in our understanding of it, is composite— a unity, not an atom. But also a unit, *a Truth*. Relatively to the range of human thought and need, it is a luminous and central *point*. As a unity, it is Theology: as a unit, a Gospel. The Gospel is, as such, the affirmation of a Divine Act of forgiveness expressed in the creative renewal of the whole man. Therefore it comes from without, and speaks of that which comes from without. Therefore also it does not place itself in line with human systems of thought and build upon the foundations of human goodness. All has to pass under the Judgement. As it is a message of re-creative Redemption, so the message itself is the implicit re-creation of human thought.

The Gnostic severance between Creation and Redemption

tends to the obliteration of both. But to this tends also all thinking that works for the reduction of them to one plane. Throughout the foregoing pages the idea of Creation, undisintegrated, has been present under, when not on, the surface. We have found it to be the tangental point between Theology and Philosophy. And our insistence on the idea of the New Creation makes a claim for *both* these words on all the emphasis that we can lay upon them. They qualify each other, it is true, but they are mutually complementary and elucidative. A few words on this point, which will recapitulate previous lines of thought in a different form, may be desirable.

Wherein does the continuity of Redemption with Creation lie, and wherein the novelty?

It is continuous in that it resumes the *purpose* of the old creation. And that means that the purpose of each is the same. If Sin had impinged upon a *completed* first creation, the very idea of Redemption would be an afterthought, with still less promise of security. For whatever further assurance its message may contain—and such it must certainly contain —it re-affirms the guarantee of Creation.

And Sin, as we have understood it, cannot be a *felix culpa*. It has no part in the causation of the Kingdom of Christ. Its entrance into God's universe is only conceivable by virtue of something indeterminate in that universe—something that has not yet realized the purpose—and that is the human will. Sin could not touch the absolutely good, and the evil would not be there. But, until man has reached his destiny, he is still imperfectly created. Grace—prevenient yet not compulsory—is not a supplement to Creation, but leads to its culmination. Therefore Redemption is itself, in respect of its aim and outcome, creative.

But it is *new* Creation. For it *resumes* the purpose. And so we get a concise formula: *continuity of purpose, discontinuity of action.* If indeed Redemption gathers up human nature in its totality—embraces the very Ego that bears that nature—

it works as truly from the foundation as creation does, therefore gathers up the whole *afresh*. Not so, as we have seen, in respect of purpose. Here it takes up a thread. But in respect of the creature, the subject of the purpose, and his resources, it takes up no thread. It does not reinforce but saves him. It is as when a man is rescued from drowning. His own faculties may not—we will suppose they do not— co-operate with his rescuer: they may even hinder him: but they are saved in his salvation. Our moral assets (as we are prone to regard them) are God's *gifts*: God's grace is God.

All this enforces the truth, alien to the Liberal tradition, that Christianity means, from end to end, intervention. The confusion of this intervention with the popular idea of miracle—an empirical event, conceivably repeatable, that "breaks" or "suspends" the laws of nature, or "contradicts experience"—is an error largely responsible for the discrediting of genuine Redemptional theology.

For that matter, it may be said, the work of any new teacher or reformer—anyone with a "message"—is an intervention. Even if he rows with the main stream of spiritual progress that is already flowing, his act of doing so is an intervention. So indeed is every act. The radical difference between a truly evangelic theology and the theologies of Continuity lies in this: whether the interventionary character of the Christian religion is taken as internal to its content and meaning, and as the pivot of its interpretation, or is merely assumed, whether the idea functions positively and actively in the thought or is otiose. The *plurality* of discontinuities that characterize the older forms of belief have naturally elicited the reaction of the "one-storey" theology. But who can measure the loss at which the correction of their errors has been won—the loss of fulcrum for our uplift, of focus to our vision, of edge to our weapons and our tools? Are we justified in naming mere exhortation and the teaching of ideas a "Gospel", not to say "*the* Gospel"? Should we not rather ask whether the supreme message entrusted to the

Church is not evangelic by its own meaning and character, not merely by the fact that it is preached? In other words, do not the giving of the message and the content of the message coincide? Is it not all God's act, directed *towards*, and therefore *through*, the human mind, therefore from outside it—outside it as the act of deliverance from the curse into which, with the whole man, it has fallen; outside it also as revealing the deliverance to eyes that, in the blindness of that curse, could never find it?

No co-operation between God transcendent and God immanent is conceivable. The more we emphasize the redeeming Act—and that as God's act—the more necessarily must we regard the God-needing creation to which it is directed as, on its highest no less than on its lowest levels, subject and material, not in any degree as co-factor. So again, in measure as we emphasize the depth and inclusiveness of human need (and the more gaping the one dimension of the void the more gaping the other), the less shall we be able to understand even our best elements in terms of such co-operation.

Two persistent demands of the human heart—demands that elicit partial or delusive response in a thousand different forms—are the demand for a practically inclusive vision and the demand for a focus for thought and life. These are in the long run inseparably connected.

These ideals are not merely theoretical: they are urgently practical. Obviously, the ordinary simple-minded person is not restive under his inability to find the first principles of mind and matter. But whenever a Beyond confronts us, an unrest tends to arise, at once from the sense of emptiness and from the sense of insecurity. Self-synthesis fails us when we cannot find our synthesis with the universe without us, and security fails when we find that the depth within us, too deep to be filled, is also too deep to be known and guarded.

Such problems would haunt us yet more but that despair

finds a shelter in ourselves, in our own thought-systems, in compromising concepts that go round and round upon the plane that itself needs the lever to raise it. To find the leverage we look beyond Time to Eternity. We get our idea of Eternity, and then it comes home to us that it is just *as* an idea—however true—that it reaches us; and, although we may believe that it is itself given to us *from* Eternity, yet it is still an idea, supported by ideas. And it is an abstract idea, with all the limitations of such. Our very mystical visitations, which are not abstractions in thought, are abstractions in experience. They are bracketed events in time, events entangled in the delusions and instabilities of physical existence.

When once we have discovered the soul as a God-created entity, with a greatness which to know is to know sin, no mere re-interpretation of the meaning of life will suffice. The situation is factual, and the answer must be factual— a Gospel.

The same thing applies essentially to the thinking man and to the average man alike. We hear a great deal about the need so to present the Christian religion that it is felt to harmonize with the characteristic mentality of the day. But disharmony comes from clash and from entanglement, not from transcendence and otherness. The vital call is to detach, to eliminate crude forms of supernaturalism, moral and psychological anthropomorphisms, ideologies and redundancies. It may be asked: does not the otherness of God, the autonomy claimed by faith, menace the mind with a cleavage which it resents? We have virtually answered this in many forms already. Such a menace would be itself a clash, not only with the perversity, but with the rightful demands, of our thought. But there is no such menace. A barrier, or a dividing space, is as such impartial in its relation to the two parties divided, and no barrier or distance exists for God, except that of sin, which He has crossed in one supreme miracle of grace. But the harmony of religion and the human intellect is not that of mere aloofness. For the intellect itself lies open, with all that we are and have, to the unique judgement of its Creator.

And then, when we consider what that revelation of God is that comes to men in that way—which alone can so come and which can come in no other way—we begin to understand how the one central inlet can admit an infinity of meaning. Initiative, self-giving, sacrifice, promise—all is taken up into the infinity of God and the immediacy of His ultimate Truth. If we could only bring home to men the implication of the essential meaning of the Gospel, as an integral whole, not after long argument and explanation but in the first instant of its impact, we—or rather it—would command the situation. Freedom from all entanglement with the uncertainties of human thinking only enhances its significance in relation to *all* thought and life, in their wholeness and at their root.

And the ideas *within* the message—the several "doctrines" —will appear as what they are, not philosophical survivals, not authoritative systems to be reverenced or despised, but as negations of negations, heading us off in the end to one luminous focal point, in the light of which they and we are to be judged. The new evangelism must address the intellect, not in the old deferential manner, but in the Name of Him who created it, and who calls on it only to be silent for a moment and to listen while He speaks.

So much for the plurality of doctrine. What of the plurality of the alleged events which express historically the Divine happening which we call Redemption? We have seen also the answer to this. They likewise are focused, and the focus is the same. The focus, in history and in idea, is the Cross; the Cross in its Divine and unique significance, the one and only paradox of religion, the descent of the Highest, the negation in the heart of the Absolute, the black sky between God and God. Then follow, by immediate necessity, the victory of the Resurrection, the pledge of the Return, the interim Kingdom and Presence of the ascended Christ, and lastly (because the knowledge of the Unique is unique knowledge) the Pentecostal Gift. None of these apart from the rest. And the whole is one simple and transcendent Fact, the moment of Time in Eternity and the moment of Eternity in Time, the Infinite that is too great to enter the realm of finite except at an indivisible point.

Thought and imagination vainly strain to understand or envisage this transcendence. But we take courage when we remember that the *infinitely* distant is the infinitely near: that the Gospel meets the very innermost soul on the basis of its two-sided need, atonement and immortality. To disparage it as a gospel of escape is to disparage the achievements of Creation that it liberates. Escape it is indeed, escape from a final death that even now has its cold hand upon the best that we are and the best that we may be, escape from the sins of refusal and denial, from hopelessness, from fear, from selfishness. And a Gift too—whatever pride and half-belief may say—the gift of eternal life in the Kingdom of Heaven, where goodness no longer lives by conflict and compromise, no longer feeds on sentiment and abstract ideals, but finds its true home in the living God, the harvest of its sacrifice in the new heaven and the new earth.

But the Gift is future first, then present. Future because faith is the substance of things *hoped for*: because these things, in their full reality, cannot be partial, cannot be veiled, cannot be mediated: because what they will be is the primary meaning of what they are. Let it be granted that, as a mundane "social gospel", this hope cannot compete with some of our optimistic dreams. Faith does not look to evolution, however it may be eked out by Evolutionism. Social reforms are the by-products of the Kingdom of God. But is not the gleaning of the grapes of Heaven better than the vintage of evolution?

The *character* formed under the conditions of renewed fellowship with the Creator is that which anticipates, in however slight a measure, for this present social order, the completed fellowship of man with man in God. The Gospel of the ultimate issue goes straight to the ultimate in man. It does not scrutinize our initial motives, but transforms them at their common root. The victory of the Resurrection and the victory of the Return join hands over our heads and beneath our feet. In the tension of the interim where we stand we cannot relapse into ineffective quietism. To live between the Divine Past of the Cross and the Divine Future of the Return is to live the eternal life amid the shadows of Time.

INDEX

For EU product safety concerns, contact us at Calle de José Abascal, 56–1°, 28003 Madrid, Spain or eugpsr@cambridge.org.

www.ingramcontent.com/pod-product-compliance
Ingram Content Group UK Ltd.
Pitfield, Milton Keynes, MK11 3LW, UK
UKHW012334130625
459647UK00009B/288